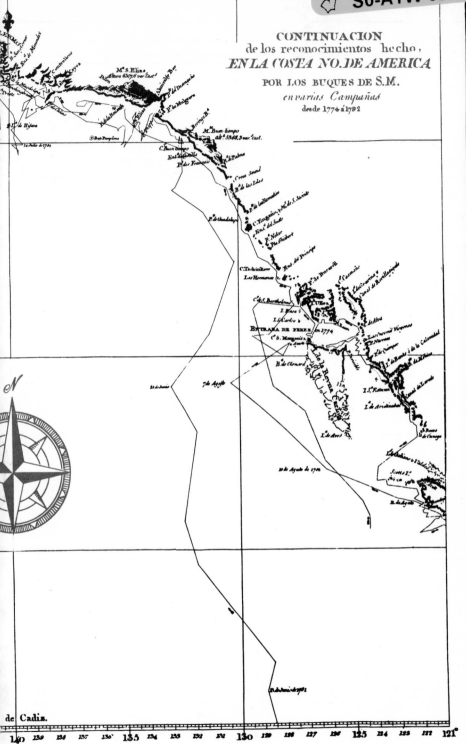

CONTINUACION
de los reconocimientos hecho,
EN LA COSTA NO. DE AMERICA
POR LOS BUQUES DE S.M.
en varias Campañas
desde 1774 á 1792

JOURNAL OF TOMÁS DE SURÍA OF HIS VOYAGE WITH

MALASPINA TO THE NORTHWEST COAST OF AMERICA IN 1791

Alejandro Malaspina - 1754-1810

JOURNAL *of* TOMÁS *de* SURÍA *of* HIS *Voyage* WITH MALASPINA *to the* NORTH-WEST COAST *of* AMERI-CA IN 1791.

TOMÁS de SURÍA

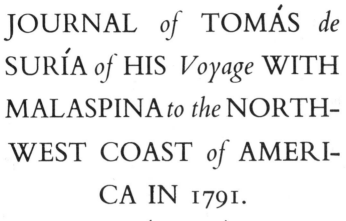

Newly Edited and with Introduction by

Donald C. Cutter

YE GALLEON PRESS
FAIRFIELD, WASHINGTON
·1980

The Henry Raup Wagner introduction and the main text of *Tomás de Suría* was reprinted from *Pacific Historical Review*, Vol. 5, No. 3, 1936, pp. 234-276, by permission of the Pacific Coast Branch, American Historical Association.

Library of Congress Cataloging in Publication Data

Suria, Tomás de, 1761-1835.
    Journal of Tomás de Suría of his voyage with Malaspina to the northwest coast of America in 1791.

    Text is reprinted from Pacific historical review, v. 5, no. 3, 1976.
    Includes bibliographical references and index.
    1. Northwest coast of North America — Discovery and exploration.
2. Indians of North America — Northwest coast of North America.
3. Suria, Tomás de, 1761-1835. 4. Malaspina, Alessandro, 1754-1809.
I. Cutter, Donald C. II. Title.
F851.5.S96   1980   970.03   80-24293
ISBN 0-87770-239-X

Table of Contents

1791

LIBRERIA DE PORRUA HERMANOS Y CIA.
Argentina y Justo Sierra.
MEXICO - 1939.

DEDICATED TO THE COURAGEOUS SPANISH GENTLEMEN

WHO EXPLORED AND MAPPED THE PACIFIC NORTHWEST

COAST OF AMERICA.

SOME NOTES

It was late June, 1791, on the Alaska coast with its longest days and shortest nights when two Spanish naval vessels sighted the prominent landmark of Mount Edgecumbe in 57° north latitude. Two years earlier these two corvettes *Descubierta* and *Atrevida* had set sail from the Spanish port of Cádiz on a projected round-the-world naval scientific exploring expedition. In overall command was the distinguished, yet still young, Captain Alejandro Malaspina, born in Mulazzo in the Spanish-held Duchy of Parma on the Italian peninsula and second son of the Count of Malaspina.

Commanding the consort vessel, the *Atrevida*, was an even younger officer of equal rank, José Bustamante y Guerra, from Santander Province in northern Spain, and a long time professional associate of Malaspina. Together the young officers had convinced the naval authorities to sponsor an all-out effort to surpass the achievements of other Western European nations which had moved ahead in the field of nautical scientific endeavor. Captain James Cook of the British Royal Navy, under the enlightened sponsorship of Sir Joseph Banks, served as the prototype with his three Pacific cruises. Jean François Galaup de La Pérouse, a French count, had commanded another worthy precursory expedition, though its disastrous end was as yet unknown to the world at the time of Malaspina's departure from Spain. Spurred by these pioneer efforts, Malaspina and Bustamante believed that Spain could compete with and surpass such European counterparts.

Virtually nothing was neglected in making ready a first-class expedition. Malaspina continually received enthusiastic support from the naval ministry, particularly from its head, Antonio Valdés y Bazán. Keels were laid for specially constructed identical twin vessels which could withstand the rigors of prolonged navigation yet be sufficiently maneuverable to carry out detailed reconnaissance in coastal waters. The resulting corvettes were 306 tons, had an overall length of 110 feet and a maximum breadth of almost 29 feet. A contemporary cutaway representation of their below decks stowage demonstrates maximum utilization of space with capacity to support the hundred officers and men assigned to each vessel. Enlisted personnel selected for the mission were hand-picked from among those best suited for extended sea duty, and the commissioned officers, midshipmen, and pilots were chosen personally by the commanders who were given almost a free hand in obtaining a suitable complement. Most of the elite officer group had previous mapping and exploring experience and most distinguished themselves not only during the 62-month cruise, but also for decades afterwards.[1]

Navigational and cartographical skills were essential to success, but other important aspects were considered from the beginning. Natural science played a major role in the initial proposal and this specialty was placed under the supervision of Antonio Pineda, an experienced officer with varied talents. Other officers, including Antonio Pineda's brother, Arcadio, did multiple duty as watch officers, astronomers, natural scientists, taxidermists, cartographers, artists, and anthropologists.

The Spanish Navy did not have officers to fill all positions needed for successful operations. A few posts went to civilians, these being highly specialized. Luis Neé, a Spaniard of French origin, served as botanist. Tadeo Haenke, a Bohemian Ph.D., M.D., was natural scientist, but with incredible versatility he did "everything." He was a linguist, musician, physician, minerologist, botanist, chemist — a Renaissance man. Finally, there were two artists, one assigned to each ship, to create the visual record of everything thought worthy of either general or scientific interest. Perspectives or general views, native types, artifacts, botanical and zoological illustrations all entered into the work of the expedition artists. Clearly the artist of yesteryear was the camera of his day, but possessed the added advantages and liabilities of the human factor in his work.

Malaspina accepted the advice of others in obtaining José del Pozo of Sevilla and José Guío of Madrid as the original artists. The former proved unsatisfactory, being characterized as lazy and undisciplined, though not without talent. He was dismissed while the exploratory vessels were along the Peruvian coast at Callao, and subsequently opened an art academy in nearby Lima. Guío was considered substandard as a result of his poor health, his inability to withstand the rigors of the sea, and his unwillingness to do other than scientific illustrations, though in this category his efforts were precise, well-executed, and eminently satisfactory.

It was the dismissal of Pozo that prompted Malaspina to write ahead to a projected future stop on his itinerary, the Viceroyalty of New Spain with its capital in Mexico City, for help in finding an artist who could serve temporarily with the expedition. More permanent arrangements for solving the artistic problem had already been instituted by writing to Europe where contracts were signed with two Italians. This pair, Juan Ravenet and Fernando Brambila, set out to intercept the exploratory group, but their arrival was not expected for several months and there was exploration to be carried out with the accompanying art work. Meanwhile a young crew member, a diminutive cabin boy from Ecija in southern Spain, began as an unofficial artist to dedicate some, and later all, of his time to drawing. He was José Cardero, who from the Ecuadorian coast northward served as "artist" and demonstrated increasing skill, so much so that in a sub-expedition of 1792 Malaspina assigned Little Pepe (Joe) to the exploratory sortie of the sloops *Sutil* and *Mexicana* that made the first circumnavigation of Vancouver Island under expedition officers Cayetano Valdés and Dionisio Alcalá-Galiano.[2]

From its inception in 1789 to 1791 the Malaspina expedition concentrated its efforts on inspection and exploration of areas within the Spanish colonies, beginning with Montevideo, Buenos Aires, Patagonia, the Malvinas, Chile, and Peru, from which point Malaspina had requested artistic reinforcement. Ahead at that time were Guayaquil, Equador; Panama; Realejo in Nicaragua; and Acapulco and San Blas on Mexico's west coast. Original plans had called for a leisurely visit to Hawaii, followed by the Northwest Coast of North America, return to Mexico, and then a trans-Pacific sailing along the outbound route of the Manila galleon to the Philippine Islands. However, Spanish diplomatic involvement with Great Britain over priorities and rights on the Northwest Coast brought about a change of operation plans. Embroilment with Britain resulted from the Nootka Sound affair in which a Spanish naval officer captured two British merchant vessels that had come to the west coast of Vancouver Island on a commercial venture. This seizure of James Colnett and his ships by Ensign Estevan José Martínez brought attention to one of the remote areas of the world, one imperfectly known geographically, but one concerning which there was an awakening of interest by several nations, principally Russia, Great Britain, United States and Spain. Of the four, Spain's interest was mostly political and hardly commercial, whereas the other three were motivated mostly by potential economic gain.

Spain believed that on the basis of early discovery and exploration it possessed exclusive rights of sovereignty, though a strong show of British diplomatic muscle was creating a reassessment. Faulty knowledge of the entire area motivated renewed reconnaissance. Prior to 1791 Spain had sent numerous exploring parties from its Mexican naval base of San Blas, and in the spring of 1790 had established an outpost at Friendly Cove, Nootka Sound. The area's labyrinth of bays, channels, islands, peninsulas and waterways was becoming better known to secretive fur traders, to Spanish naval officers, and to British explorers, but there still remained a lingering doubt about the possible existence of a long hoped for strait through North America. If one existed, Spain wanted to be the first to find it and possess it for the political advantage that would result.

It was for good reasons, all of them concerned with Spanish claims and rights of sovereignty, that Malaspina's ships were dispatched by royal order in the summer of 1791 to the northern latitudes. Malaspina was told to skip the projected visit to Hawaii and to scour the coast for a strait, more specifically for one thought to have been found in 1588 by Lorenzo Ferrer Maldonado, a supposed Spanish navigator whose apocryphal account of a waterway had recently gained credence in European scientific circles. Malaspina was also ordered to perform acts of sovereignty by a more modern abbreviated method than the antiquated protracted rituals of possession. By doing this Spain would insure its existing claims and strengthen future pretensions to the area. He was also instructed to visit and report upon the Spanish settlement in the process of construction at Nootka, and while there to investigate first hand the basis for Spanish claim which rested in part on primacy of contact, supported by earlier acts of possession, and finally on permanent settlement with Indian consent. Malaspina's inquiry was to be accompanied by map making, drawing of coastal profiles as aids to navigation, scientific experiments, astronomical observations, and efforts to understand and win the confidence of the local natives with special attention to gratifying the Nootka chief, Maquinna.[3]

It was as a temporary substitute for the deposed José del Pozo that Mexican artist-engraver Tomás de Suría joined the Spanish naval scientists for the Pacific Northwest phase of that expedition under circumstances described below. In some regards this part of the trip was extraordinary, for it was the first time that the group examined territory over which Spain had no effective sovereignty. The explorers were entering an area in which they could count on little by way of local informants to supplement their direct observation. It was only the second time that the entire group had intensive contact with uncivilized aborigines. It also marked the first time that expedition activities could have international ramifications.

While aboard the *Descubierta* under the direct command of

10

Malaspina, Suría wrote a journal which translated into English forms the body of this book. From his own comments, the artist was not encouraged to keep an account and was even deprived of the opportunity of comparing his comments with those of the ship's officers who kept authorized journals. Although Suría bemoaned this literary isolation from official sources, today his account serves to amplify our knowledge, since the artist's parallel diary has considerable material not contained in any of the official versions. Furthermore, Suría's diary is interspersed by his drawings and by explanations of things and events graphically portrayed. The decision, probably made by Malaspina, to deny Suría access to official expedition accounts was seemingly made to prevent substantial leakage of findings before publication of what was intended to be a well organized, comprehensive report in many volumes of text. Wise as this decision may have been in 1791, the artist was definitely annoyed. For example, he asserted that his observation of Indian life was realistic and not romanticized as were the official accounts. Suría's diary was never published during his lifetime nor for a century afterward, and Malaspina's great compendium was for political reasons never even close to publication, though one version, that of Lieutenant Francisco Javier de Viana, appeared in 1849 sponsored by his sons.[4] Of all the accounts, and they were multiple and usually repetitious, Suría's was the only private one, and it possesses the freshness and naiveté of a landlubber afloat. It is also the diary of a person who was in the flush of enthusiasm for his work and in his writing.

The original Suría journal is today in the Coe Collection of Yale University Library. Before its present resting place at New Haven, the journal was available to the famous Hispanist and bibliophile Henry Raup Wagner. Author of several works on Spain on the Pacific Coast, Wagner published a translation of the artist's diary as "The Journal of Tomás de Suría of his Voyage with Malaspina to the Northwest Coast of America in 1791" in the *Pacific Historical Review*, September, 1936. His translation was supported by his own annotations supplemented by anthropological notes by W.A. ("Billy") Newcombe. Both Wagner's notes and those of Newcombe are of lasting value and the former's translation efforts were largely satisfactory.

In 1939, without access to the original journal, Justino Fernández in Mexico City produced a small book entitled *Tomás de Suría y su viaje con Malaspina, 1791* in an edition limited to 500 copies. Fernández translated back into Spanish the Wagner translation, preserved most of the footnotes, added a few of his own, but did his greatest service in providing introductory information concerning Suría and his role in Mexico's art history. In the present introduction Fernández's contributions are summarized.

More recently, in 1972, Agueda Jiménez Pelayo of Guadalajara, utilizing microfilm of the original journal, Wagner's translation, Justino Fernández' study, as well as several expedition journals and guardbooks, wrote a master's thesis for University of New Mexico "Tomás de Suría y su participación en la expedición al Noroeste de América," but done in Mexico in the University of New Mexico—Universidad Autónoma de Guadalajara Master Plan program in history. This thesis, done under my direction, has been of help to me in formulating this introduction and I acknowledge my debt to Señorita Jiménez.

The decision of Ye Galleon Press has been to make again available Wagner's translation, with this new introduction and added notes which incorporate new and old data on the artist, the expedition and associated bibliography. New notes for the Wagner translation are numbered rather than lettered, while supplementary material to preexisting notes is found at the end. Additions within the text are made by the present editor utilizing square brackets. All notes in the Wagner introduction are made by the present editor.

Tomás de Suría, whose journal adds dimensions to the Malaspina story, was born in Spain in April, 1761, probably in Madrid, to Francisco de Suría and Feliciana Lozano. As a student at the Royal Art Academy of San Fernando, the young artist came under the tutelage of Jerónimo Antonio Gil, an art figure of some standing in Spain. At age 17, the youth was invited to accompany his mentor to Mexico where Gil was sent to found the Academy of San Carlos. Suría later laid exaggerated claim to having been one of the two founders of that Mexican art center which is still in existence in the capital.[5] In addition to his connection with the academy, the youthful student began work as a designer at the mint.

On December 15, 1788, Suría married María Josefa Fernández de Mendoza, daughter of Joaquín Fernández and Josefa Molina. By 1791 he was thirty years old, had two children, and resided in the same household as his in-laws in the viceregal capital. Upon receipt by Viceroy Conde de Revilla Gigedo of the letter Malaspina had written from Guayaquil, that important Mexican dignitary sought with eagerness a person expert in drawing and perspective to accompany the scientists.[6] In his efforts the Viceroy wrote to the president of the directive committee of the Royal Academy, Ramón Posada, to obtain from among the most advanced and expert of San Carlos the person who would volunteer under the conditions predetermined by Malaspina. Posada in turn wrote to Adacemy Director Gil who transmitted news of the opportunity to the academy membership.

Suría was one of four who responded favorably, but only two were considered by Gil to be sufficiently competent. They were José María Guerrero and Suría and each indicated the terms under which he would go. The latter's note said that he had consulted his wife who approved, and that he would go provided he kept his job with its salary, was guaranteed his senority of twelve years, and would suffer no prejudice in subsequent promotion. He asked for a salary of from 1500 to 2000 pesos, travel expenses until his return, along with suitable quarters and food.

Revilla Gigedo left the decision to Posada who chose Suría "as an apt person, the most suitable of those available." He had been more modest in his demands than had Guerrero, but even so the winning candidate requested an advance and "first-class" mess. After some negotiating on terms, Suría was accepted by the Viceroy and his employer at the mint was notified.

All was done hurriedly including obtaining advance pay, passport, drawing paper and art supplies, so that Suría might get to Acapulco by February 8. One last problem arose when the artist's wife and mother-in-law lodged a vigorous protest against his going, first to Posada and subsequently directly to the viceroy. The complaint, which was motivated out of love and because of the good standing that the artist had with his in-laws, came to naught except possibly to insure prompt subsequent payment of his regular monthly salary directly to his wife.

Prior to departure from Mexico City, Suría requested the loan of a popular art textbook by Antonio Palomino de Castro on the theory and practice of painting, and that he be given prints of marine views. The former was facilitated on condition of its subsequent return, but the latter were not available. Anyhow, it was felt that during the expedition the artist would have more than enough marine views.[7]

The new expedition artist did not reach Acapulco until February 16, two weeks after arrival of the *Atrevida*, commanded by Bustamante. The artist reported to the subordinate commander, but was not accepted aboard because of lack of billeting space.[8] He was told to remain ashore until arrival of the *Descubierta*. On March 27 the command vessel entered Acapulco and Suría reported aboard bearing a letter of presentation from the viceroy who characterized the artist "as a very honorable young man, of complete aptitude,...the most useful of any available."⁹ Malaspina promptly assigned the newcomer to work under the orders of the Chief of Natural History, Antonio Pineda. While at Acapulco Suría turned his hand to a type of art that was new to him, a brief series of zoological drawings which were sent off the Spain almost immediately. These, united with others done by José Guío and José Cardero, were forwarded to Madrid before departure for the Northwest Coast. A list of these was made by Pineda and all except one can be found today in the Museo Naval of the Spanish Ministry of Marine in Madrid. Five were land animals and seven were fish. Some bear the characteristic Latin autograph *Suría Fecit*.¹⁰ Even this first work brought forth praise from the expedition commander.

On May 1, the *Descubierta* and *Atrevida,* with Suría aboard the former, set sail for northern latitudes in a vain search for the Strait of Ferrer Maldonado. Following well-established precedent, the vessels sailed far westward before heading north, so as to miss the prevailing northwesterlies of the coast. As a result of their chosen track the ships were out of sight of land for over fifty days.

Suría's journal is its own best interpreter, but will also be supported by the notes of Wagner, Newcombe and myself. The original journal was probably in two parts with the first portion still extant. The Yale manuscript has "Primer Cuaderno," or "First Notebook" on the cover, implying the existence of a "segundo," but not guarantying it. If a second exists or existed, its fate is unknown; but the abrupt termination while at Nootka about half way through his voyage suggests that Suría had only two rather than more notebooks. In Justino Fernández' book published in Mexico in 1939, he utilized some other Malaspina expedition accounts to piece together the entire northern cruise including the rest of the stay at Nootka and the subsequent visit to California's capital of Monterey.

In more recent times the Suría account, at least the portion concerning Port Mulgrave in Yakutat Bay, Alaska, was used extensively by Frederica de Laguna in her anthropological study of the local Indians entitled *Under Mount Saint Elias: The History and Culture of the Yakutat Tlinget* (Washington, 1972). The author was under the mistaken impression that Suría was the sole Spanish artist at Mulgrave in 1791 and therefore erroneously ascribes many drawings, even those bearing

Cardero's autograph, to Suria.

Warren Cook in *Floodtide of Empire: Spain and the Pacific Northwest, 1543-1819* (New Haven, 1973) is the only other author to use Suria's account to any appreciable extent. Cook had access to the Yale manuscript and had a much greater knowledge of written Spanish than anthropologist de Laguna.

In writing his journal aboard the *Descubierta*, the Mexican artist was in close association with Second Pilot Joaquín Hurtado with whom he was quartered in a very small compartment, and with Felipe Bauzá y Cañas, a native of Mallorca who served the expedition as Chief of Charts and Maps or Geographer, as they more frequently called him. Years later Bauzá became custodian and conservator of much of the Malaspina material. He also kept one of the several authorized journals, one in which he mentions Suria with some frequency, as do other expedition chroniclers.[11] Curiously, José Cardero, former cabin boy who became unofficial artist sailing aboard the *Atrevida*, is never mentioned by Suria and infrequently mentioned by others until after the Northwest Coast phase was completed.

Suria was at times inaccurate in use of names, but was no worse nor better than other Malaspina personnel in this regard. His impressions as a novice at sea were sincere and naive, but the very fact that he was chosen and accepted the challenge are considerable recommendations for his capacity. Certainly no other account has the spice of his rough sketches that add greatly to the merit of the Mexican artist's participation. He carried out his work under both favorable and unfavorable conditions with the result that in addition to his journal we have several dozen drawings as the result of his participation.

Upon return to Acapulco, the artist-engraver completed his contracted service. After the arrival of Malaspina the two Italian artists appeared, thereby making not only Suria but also Cardero surplus beyond expedition requirements. A report in the press commented on the fine job that Suria had done and assured readers that

> Some day the data will be presented to the public with the accompanying map and a beautiful collection of precise drawings done by Don Tomás de Suria, from which a complete idea can be formed of not only the scientific works and the different happenings during their stay in those parts but also of the physiognomy, dress, dwellings, and utensils of those inhabitants.[12]

In a letter Malaspina requested that the Viceroy permit Suria to work for the next six months preparing finished copies of such work as remained

15

incomplete. Revilla Gigedo acceded to this request and Suría spent not six but eight months in the task since the Viceroy gave permission to have the artist work for as long as necessary.

Again from Acapulco more drawings were forwarded to Spain. These consisted of "the drawings of Don Tomás Suría and of José Cardero of the most important objects of the most recent campaign. Those which have been done in pencil have been placed under glass so as not to become smudged. Some have not been finished yet which are being done in final copies."[13]

A resume of Malaspina's satisfaction with Suría's artistic performance was included in a letter written to the Viceroy: "At this time it has seemed to me proper to assure Your Excellency as I am now doing that this able subject has lived up completely to your correct opinion."[14] At the same time, Malaspina wrote to his superior, Naval Minister Valdés: "Finally our collections for the Royal Museum have been numerous and very interesting inasmuch as Don Tomás Suría has depicted with the greatest fidelity to nature all that merits the help of the engraver's art, so as to secure better understanding in the historical narrative of this voyage."[15]

For years Suría used his early connection with the expedition to attempt to gain preferment. As early as June 21, 1794 he complained bitterly about his poor situation, being sick and without means, and asking a promotion or a transfer since for sixteen years he had served in the mint without having had any promotion. He also asked that he be given a certificate verifying his participation in the trip to the Northwest Coast with Malaspina. Revilla Gigedo apparently did not respond with anything more than the desired certificate which was issued by Viceregal Secretary Colonel Antonio Bonilla.[16] Consequently, Suría remained in his position as engraver until the death of his mentor, Gil, in 1798 at which time the position of chief engraver was given to Suría.

In 1805 Suría held the position of regular pay accountant, third class, but also continued with his art work, much of which was of a religious nature. Eight of these later efforts are reproduced in the book *Tomás de Suría*...by Justino Fernández, which also contains a listing of other known works including his last, a pencil sketch "The Resurrection of Lazarus," done in 1834 at a time when Suría's eyesight was failing.[17]

In the interval Suría became occupied in the engraving of medallions dealing with royal political affairs. However, he seems to have been in the mid-current of change involved with Mexican independence, as well as in minor political activities of the independent government under Agustín Iturbide. In the first year of independence Suria served under that short-lived regime as secretary of a committee dealing with reforms of government in Lower and Upper California, that is, what are today the Mexican areas of Baja California Sur, Baja California Norte and the U.S. State of California. Subsequently the artist served as Secretary of the Committee of the Californias and was known to be in possession of Jesuit documents from the period before the expulsion of that order from New Spain in 1767. Perhaps Suria's fifteen day stay in Monterey with Malaspina in September of 1791 made him an authority. At any rate, he seems not to have suffered in independent Mexico from the fact that he had been born in Europe, as was the case with many peninsular Spaniards.

Suria is thought to have died in 1835 without great recognition. But he certainly was better appreciated than Malaspina, the commander whom he served. The expedition leader after his return to Spain in 1794 was at first lionized but was later swept aside in a vortex of political intrigue that brought him to a sad end. He was tried on trumped up charges of subversion and found guilty. The court remanded him to a gloomy military prison at San Antón, a rocky island in the Bay of La Coruña. There he spent eight years until his sentence was commuted to banishment to his native land. In 1810 in the home of a baker in Pontremoli, in Italy, the once prominent Malaspina died an obscure death. Almost as forgotten were the results of his sixty-two month expedition until recent travelling museum exhibits and well-illustrated publications have brought forth belated recognition of Malaspina as a worthy colleague of the better known Cook and La Pérouse.[18] With realization of Malaspina's historical importance, Tomás de Suria also becomes better appreciated for his journalistic and artistic contributions to early regional history.

In summary, Suria clearly reached the peak of his historical importance in his association with Malaspina's "round-the-world" naval scientific exploring group, but he was unable to use that connection to vault into great prominence. His interlude with Captain Malaspina neither aided nor detracted greatly from his career. It has been only recently with an awakening of interest in Malaspina and his scientific cruise that Suria has been rescued from near oblivion, for both as artist and journalist of regional history his role as a pioneer figure is clear. Republication of his journal by Ye Galleon Press after over forty years since its discovery by

Wagner, and almost two centuries since his work was accomplished, is a belated tribute to a notable Hispanic contributor to Pacific Northwest Coast history.

Donald C. Cutter, Ph.D.
March 24, 1980
Professor of History, University of New Mexico
Albuquerque, New Mexico

FOOTNOTES TO CUTTER INTRODUCTION

1. Pedro de Novo y Colson (ed.), *Viaje político-científico alrededor del mundo por las corbetas Descubierta y Atrevida* . . . (1885) contains a summary of preparations and of execution of the entire voyage.

2. Donald C. Cutter, "Spanish Artists on the Northwest Coast," in *Pacific Northwest Quarterly*, Vol. 54. Oct. 1963.

3. Antonio Valdéz to Malaspina, Madrid, December 22, 1790 in Malaspina Correspondence, Vol. I, MS 278 in Museo Naval.

4. Francisco Javier de Viana, *Diario del viage explorador de las Corbetas Españolas Descubierta y Atrevida en los años de 1789 a 1794* (Cerrito de la Victoria, 1849).

5. Suría to Andrés Mendivil, Mexico, February 28, 1826, in Archivo de la Antigua Academia de San Carlos, Mexico City, MS #1962.

6. Revillà Gigedo to Pedro de Lerena, Mexico, January 15, 1791, in Archivo General de Indias, Sevilla, Audiencia de Mexico 1540.

7. Correspondence relative to the selection of Suría and of preparations for his trip are found in Archivo General de la Nación, Mexico, (AGN), Historia, tomo 397.

8. Diario del Comandante de la Atrevida [Bustamante], MS 271 in Museo Naval.

9. Revilla Gigedo to Malaspina, Mexico, January 19, 1791 in AGN, Historia 397.

10. Lista de los Dibujos concluidos...dibujados por Suría in Pineda, Nueva España, MS 1563 in Museo Naval.

11. Felipe Bauzá, Viaje alrededor del Mundo, 1789-96, MSS 749-50 in Museo Naval.

12. *Gaceta de Mexico*, December 1791

13. The contents of this shipment are listed in AGN, Historia 277 and in Bauzá, Viaje...MS 750.

14. Malaspina to Viceroy, Acapulco, November 1, 1791 in AGN, Historia 397.

15. Malaspina to Antonio Valdés, San Blas, October 12, 1791 and quoted in Cutter, *Malaspina in California*, (San Francisco, 1960, p. 15).

16. This correspondence is in AGN, Historia 397.

17. Justino Fernández, *Tomás de Suría y su viaje con Malaspina, 1791*, (Mexico, 1939), pp. 106-27.

18. *The Malaspina Expedition: "In the Pursuit of Knowledge..."* (Santa Fe, Mueum of New Mexico Press, 1977); *Voyages of Enlightenment: Malaspina on the Northwest Coast, 1791/1792* (Portland, Oregon Historical Society, 1977); and Donald C. Cutter, "The Return of Malaspina" in *The American West*, Jan.-Feb., 1978, pp. 4-19.

Jose de Bustamante y Guerra

Introduction

After the conclusion of the peace with England in 1783, the Spanish government set on foot a series of explorations by land and sea with the object of improving their maps and especially their hydrographic maps. After some exploration in the Atlantic it was decided that it was necessary to improve the general map of the west coast of North and South America. September 10, 1788, Alejandro Malaspina and José Bustamante y Guerra, both commanders in the royal navy, proposed a scientific voyage around the world with two corvettes. Besides the geographical objects of the proposed voyage, an investigation of the political state of Spanish America, relative to Spain, and that of other nations, was to be made, which would include not only the collection of curiosities, plants, etc., but also of statistics of the productions of the various countries. The plan was approved by the king and two new corvettes of about 300 tons each were constructed under the direct supervision of Malaspina himself. The vessels sailed from Cadiz July 30, 1789. Malaspina was in command of the *Descubierta* and Bustamante of the *Atrevida*. Scientists were numerous, Antonio Pineda, Felipe Bauzá,[1] Luis Neé, Tadeo Haenke, and some others. Two painters accompanied the expedition, José del Pozo and José Guio.

It was not until February and March, 1791, that the two vessels reached Acapulco, Mexico. Here two astronomers joined them, José Espinosa y Tello and Ciriaco Zevallos.[2] Meanwhile both of Malaspina's painters had become sick and left the expedition. Two others, Fernando Brambila and Juan Ravenet, were ordered to proceed from Spain[3] and join him, but in the meantime, urgent orders came to explore the northwest coast, and Tomás de Suría, a painter living in Mexico, was appointed by the viceroy to fill the place. Suría's journal, the translation of which we are publishing, contains a passably good account of the voyage until the arrival at Nootka and it is not necessary to make a summary of the voyage at this point. Suffice it to say that Malaspina's vessels sailed from Acapulco May 1, 1791, and sighted the coast in latitude 56° 17' on June 23. From here Malaspina proceeded to Yakutat Bay. A most interesting account of this has been preserved for us by Suría which differs in some respects from the official narrative.

21

The object of this hurried expedition to the northwest coast was to see if a passage to the Atlantic could be found as described by Lorenzo Ferrer Maldonado, who claimed to have passed through it from the Atlantic in 1588. This passage, which he called the Estrecho de Anian, was stated by him to lie in 60º. Therefore when the expedition reached Yakutat Bay a search for the passage began. Malaspina had high hopes that at the east end of this bay such a passage would be found but a boat expedition soon destroyed the delusion. From here Malaspina sailed west without approaching the coast very closely until near Cape Suckling. He only reached as far west as Hinchinbrook Island and did not enter Prince William Sound. As a matter of fact by this time he was convinced that no such strait existed and therefore became very lukewarm in the search for it. On the 27th of July he gave up his search for the strait and began his return voyage along the coast. He finally reached Nootka August 12, and after making some astronomical observations sailed on August 28 and on September 12 entered Monterey Bay. October 10 he anchored in San Blas. From here he made his way westward to Manila,[4] examined the Philippine Islands and then visited Botany Bay. After some exploration in this neighborhood and the South Sea islands the expedition returned to Callao and from there by way of Cape Horn to Spain.

A great mass of material relating to this voyage still remains unpublished, much of it in what was known as the Depósito Hydrográfico but which now forms a part of the collection in the Museo Naval.[5] The first publication of the voyage to the northwest coast occurs in an "Examen histórico-crítico de los viajes y descubrimientos apócrifos del Capitan Lorenzo Ferrer Maldonado, de Juan de Fuca y del Almirante Bartolomé de Fonte." This memoir was begun by Martín Fernández de Navarrete and concluded after his death by his son. It was published in 1849 in Tomo XV of the *Colección de Documentos Inéditos para la Historia de España*. In 1884 Captain Pedro de Novo y Colson published the *Viaje político-científico alrededor del mundo por las corvetas Descubierta y Atrevida*. An account of the northwest expedition contained in the latter is somewhat different from that contained in Navarrete; they were probably written by different members of the expedition.

Suría was born at Valencia in or about April, 1761, according to the researches made at my request by my friend Don Federico Gómez de Orozco.[6] In 1778 he came to Mexico with Jerónimo Gil who had been appointed director of the school of engraving in Mexico City. Gil took possession of the position December 24 of that year and on the same day Suría was placed in the mint in the engraving office. Nothing more is known of him until he was selected by the viceroy to accompany Malaspina to the northwest coast in 1791. Malaspina on his return to Acapulco wrote to the viceroy November 1 highly recommending him. In a letter written by Suría June 11, 1794, relating his services he states that after his return to Mexico he spent eight months in putting his sketches into proper shape. He remained at work in the mint until November 25, 1806, when he was appointed an auditor of payments of the third class. In 1813 he was still living according to a memorial of his of that year. Señor Gómez de Orozco has not been able to ascertain when he died. He was skilled in engraving and Señor Orozco has a medal engraved by him on the occasion of the taking of the oath in Mexico to Fernando VII, also two engravings in the works of Alcocer and Bartolache.[7]

Suría's final sketches of which he speaks in his letter of 1794 were no doubt sent to Madrid and added to the mass of material accumulated by Malaspina to be used in his great contemporary work on the Spanish colonial possessions. How much of this remains is uncertain but no doubt much of it has disappeared or been mislaid. The Museo Naval has some of Suría's sketches, perhaps all. When the account of the Malaspina expedition was published by the Spanish government in 1884, the sketch made by Suría of the sepulchre in Port Mulgrave was included (page 120).[8] Various references occur in the text to his sketching Ankau, the sepulchre, a large house, and various scenes in Port Mulgrave and the sketching of the chiefs at Nootka. A number of his sketches have been reproduced recently by the Museo Naval in Madrid in a volume entitled *Reportorio de los mss., Cartas, planos y dibujos relativos a las Californias existentes en este Museo* (Madrid, 1932).

Allowing for errors in assigning Suría sketches to Brambila who was never north of Acapulco, and to Cordero who never saw the far northwest coast,[9] we find the following by him reproduced:

Vista de la pira y sepulcro del actual jefe de Mulgrave. . . . . VI[10]
Vista de la Bahia de Desengaño. . . . . IX[11]
Apunte de una Mujer de Mulgrave. XII
Apunte de una Mujer de Mulgrave XIII
    (the title is in Suría's handwriting)
Indio de Mulgrave. XIV
    (the title is in Suría's handwriting)

    (Plate XII is our Plate No. 2 and Plate XIV is our No. 1.)

In addition to the above I am inclined to attribute to him Plate IV — Vista del presidio de Monterey,[12] and Plate XI — India de Monterey, although in the *Reportorio* this is attributed to Cardero [that is, Cordero] and may possibly have been drawn by him as he was there in 1792.

The most interesting plate in the book is Plate V on which is written, and not in Suría's handwriting: "Resibimiento del Conde de la Pei Rus en la Mision del Carmelo de Monterei." This is attributed to Brambila, but incorrectly. Malaspina himself (page 197 of the *Viaje*) states that he found this picture in the mission and that it had been painted by M. Duché de Vancy of the La Pérouse expedition. H.H. Bancroft, in his *History of California*,[13] has an interesting account of the later history of this sketch, which was given away in 1833. Of one thing we may be fairly certain, and that is, that the friars of the mission did not allow Malaspina to carry it away. I therefore conclude that the one in the Museo Naval is a copy made by Suría.[14] Besides those I have mentioned, the sketches of the chiefs in Nootka, Maquina and Clupaneta, are also in the Museo Naval and the one entitled "Modo del pelear los Indios de California" is also probably by Suría although attributed to Brambila.[15] It is not unlikely also that the Nootka sketches reproduced in the atlas to the *Viaje de las goletas Sutil y Mexicana*, published in Madrid in 1802,[16] are by Suría. There seems to be some vague reference in the text of the Malaspina voyage to the *Oratorio del Tais* in the same work as having been drawn by him.

The manuscript belongs to Mr. W.R. Coe of New York City. He has given me his kind permission to translate and publish it and in addition had paid the expense of having the plates made. It is greatly to be regretted that the journal is incomplete. Not only are several leaves relating to the stay in Nootka misplaced but several have been lost including what we must suppose to have been the observations of Suría on the last few days' stay in Nootka after his return from the boat expedition. What we deplore the most is the absence of his account of the visit to Monterey. As the present document is entitled "Primer Cuaderno" it is possible that the latter part of the voyage after leaving Nootka may have been continued in a "Segundo Cuaderno." Both the title and the cover contain the word "Reservado" and the one on the cover adds the word "con juramento," that is, "sworn." Unfortunately in later years Suría, who had become almost blind, scribbled mostly unintelligible words on the blank pages and in one case over almost a complete page. They generally seem to have some connection with his bad eyes, but in some cases he has attempted to describe the sketches. He makes much of his difficulty in obtaining information about the navigation from the officers and pilots but in one case he has inserted several pages which are practically an exact copy of part of the log of some one of the officers which was published in the *Viaje* in 1884.

In conclusion I may say that this is the only unofficial journal with one exception that I have ever seen of any of the Spanish voyages to the northwest coast and the frank expression of his opinions, which would not be tolerated in an official journal, adds intense interest to his account.

I wish to extend my thanks to Don Federico Gómez de Orozco for information regarding Suría, and to Mr. W.A. Newcombe, of Victoria, for his ethnographical notes to the narrative. These are designated at the end by N.

HENRY R. WAGNER

San Marino, California

Tomás de Suría

FOOTNOTES FOR WAGNER INTRODUCTION

by Dr. Donald Cutter

1. Bauzá is the true spelling, and he was not a scientist, but rather the son of a brick-layer who had worked his way through the pilotage corps to a navy commission as ensign. His proficiency as an artist might have qualified him in that area.

2. Though both José Espinosa y Tello and Ciriaco Cevallos (not Zevallos) were proficient in taking astronomical observations, neither was strictly-speaking an astronomer.

3. Fernando Brambila and Juan Francisco de Ravenet y Bunel were both Italians and had been contracted in Italy.

4. Via Guam in the Marianas Islands.

5. Many of the drawings and artifacts are today in the Museo de América in Madrid. Specimens concerned with natural history are still awaiting study in the Archivo del Real Jardín Botánico. Other expedition materials are in the Museo de Ciencias Naturales, at Yale University, and in the British Museum.

6. No other evidence has been presented for Valencia as the birth place of Suría.

7. Lists of Suría's works are in Justino Fernández, *Tomás de Suría y su viaje con Malaspina*, pp. 115-23.

8. But this was done by unofficial expedition artist José Cardero who sailed aboard the *Atrevida*. Wagner insistently calls him Cordero.

9. Cardero was definitely at Mulgrave and Nootka. He returned to the Northwest Coast a year later with the voyage of the sloops *Sutil* and *Mexicana*, visiting Nootka, circumnavigating Vancouver Island and stopping over at Monterey on his way home.

10. Done by Cardero.

11. Done later by Italian artist Juan Ravenet from an earlier sketch, probably by Cardero.

12. Done by Cardero or by Brambila using Cardero's earlier sketch.

13. Vol. I, pp. 432-33.

14. There were at least three drawings. All three appear in Donald C. Cutter, *Malaspina in California* (San Francisco, 1960), following p. 42.

15. Provisionally attributed to Cardero. Cutter, *Malaspina*, p. 17.

16. This work in two volumes has been republished in 1958 by José Porrua Turanzas (Madrid).

JOURNAL OF TOMÁS DE SURÍA OF HIS VOYAGE WITH

MALASPINA TO THE NORTHWEST COAST OF AMERICA IN 1791

On the 16th of February, 1791, I reached the Port of Acapulco, distant from the capital of Mexico 110 leagues, made up as follows:

From Mexico to Cuernavaca	18 leagues
From Cuernavaca to Puente de Ystla	9 leagues
From Puente de Ystla to the Amates	12 leagues
From the Amates to Santa Teresa	11 leagues
From Santa Teresa to Sumpango	16 leagues
From Sumpango to Chilpancingo	3 leagues
From Chilpancingo to Quajiniguilapa	10 leagues
From Quajiniguilapa to Peregrino	11 leagues
From Peregrino to the Atajo	12 leagues
From Atajo to Acapulco	8 leagues
Total	110 Spanish leagues

Note: This road is all through very broken country with the exception of three plains.

The corvette *Atrevida* anchored in this port February 2, commander Don José Bustamante y Guerra,[1] *capitan de fragata* of the royal armada and *segundo comandante* and the first of the *corveta*, a *caballero* of the Cross of Santiago.[2] He made his astronomical observations and sounded the port and the bay. The botanist of the vessel, Don Luis•Neé,[3] a very famous Frenchman, went about the country botanizing and found a plant called *"Mimosa sensitiva"* which has the faculty of closing its leaves when touched and then opening them again. In Figure 1a, they are seen opened, in Figure 2a, closed.[4] The sketches of plants they brought back for this branch of science were fairly well done but nothing more.

Sail was made on the 26th of February for San Blas, where they were to build a longboat, for which purpose and for any others for which they might be needed some artisans and various experts were carried.[5]

March 27 the corvette *Descubierta*, commander, Don Alejandro Malaspina, *capitan de navio* of the royal navy and a *caballero* of the Cross of Malta, came in. She anchored in front of the castle of San Diego and in the night was towed in until she was moored by a cable to the silk-cotton tree on the beach. Its form is the following. [Figure][6]

On the 28th I commenced work under the order of First Lieutenant of Marines, Don Antonio Pineda,[7] who is in charge of the section of Natural History, and up to the 29th of the following April I had drawn various fish, birds, quadrupeds, and the anatomy of animals, which I delivered to the commander as he had asked me for them for the shipment he was about to make to the court of all that had been done.[8]

May 1 we set sail at 10:30 for the north. From this day the wind favored us, although but little during the first days. Afterwards it kept freshening and we came to make on some days six miles (per hour). The first course was to the south until the 4th of May, then to the west until the 14th, and now we take a course to the northeast.

Today the 19th we are on the Tropic of Cancer.[9] Up to today the best precautions have been taken on board for the purpose of preventing any kind of contagious disease such as is usually encountered in this sailing to the north. Our commander has ordered the sailors to clean ship three times, making them take out their clothing and the rest of their luggage from between decks.and put it on top of the boat and longboat in order to ventilate it. Likewise the doctor, Don Francisco Flores, has the task of finding out by means of the eudiometer what degree of malignity is contained in the air of the ship from the hold up, in order to make useful regulations to secure the conservation of the health of our crew which so far continued without change.

Yesterday the troops were passed in review with their arms and clothing and performed their exercise on the quarter deck. The commander, knowing well that we were going to certain places where there are Indians but little civilized and fierce, had taken good precautions for whatever might occur. He has named the men who are to take part in the expeditions with the longboat. These are very vigorous, most of them Galicians and some Andalusians, and Don Cayetano Valdés[10] is to command them. The longboat was well equipped in Acapulco to withstand these campaigns, two doors being opened in the stern for the ventilation of the·small cabin. The arms which the men will carry are a gun, two pistols, a cutlass, and a knife.

From the 20th we began to experiment on the air in the boatswain's room and in this sixty parts of good air out of 100 were found. Introduced in the eudiometer of Abbé Fontana,[11] with an equal quantity of nitrous gas, the mixture resulted in sixty per cent of wholesomeness. On performing the same task in the storeroom fifty-seven per cent of pure air was found, a difference which the doctor attributed to the corruptible materials kept in the storeroom whose fermentation infected the air. A corresponding experiment was also performed on the atmospheric air and that between decks, the result being that what was between decks was healthier than that of the atmosphere to the extent of five parts. The doctor thought this was on account of the neighborhood of the cookstove in the kitchen which purified the air.

The winds continue quite fresh, although they have moderated somewhat in the last three days. We make three or four miles per hour and are in 24° of latitude.

On the 21st the ship was hove to and the commander ordered the boat to be put in the water. This was done and Don Cayetano Valdés, Don Secundino Salamanca,[12] the purser, Don Rafael de Arias,[13] and Don Tadeo Kaeink [hereafter correctly spelled "Haenke"],[14] the botanist, went alongside the *Atrevida*. From the *Atrevida* the same proceeding was followed and Don Fabio Aliponzoni,[15] the father chaplain and the surgeon came to our ship.[16] Our commander did this for the purpose of giving out various instructions on the procedure of our voyage to the commander of the *Atrevida*. For this purpose they exchanged some geographical maps of the regions of the north to which we were going and also instructions were issued about how to combine the daily observations for latitude and longitude of the two corvettes. Today we are in 25° and some minutes of latitude, continuing a course northeast. The sun sets at 7 o'clock and the angelus was given at 7:30.

On the 22nd the wind strengthened and we made four miles, and there is some swell. We are in 26° of latitude. The experiments on the air were continued by the doctor. Some came from the *Atrevida* in their boat because their chronometer had gotten out of order.

On the 23d we made two and one-third miles, the wind light, latitude 27½°. Our commander ordered the gunner to exercise the troops with the cannon and this was begun today.

The 24th, almost calm, latitude 28°.

The 25th, we continued with but little wind.

The 26th, it dawned very clear and serene, but calm. In view of this state of affairs the commander ordered a repetition of the cannon exercise for the crew and soldiers. This was done and they are growing expert; the same was done with the guns and pistols. This exercise and that with the cannon was repeated almost every day, therefore we refrain from referring to it again. Latitude 29^0, wind fresh, although light.

On the same day, while calm, the boat of the *Atrevida* came with the commander and officers, leaving only the man who was on watch. A splendid breakfast was served during which there was chatter appropriate to such a place and such occasions. Mr. Haenke played on the harpsichord with his accustomed skill. After it was over they returned to their ship.

The 27th, the calm continued.

The 28th, there was some breeze, but very light.

The 29th, it freshened a little more so that we made two miles per hour which enabled us during these days to make a degree of latitude.

On the 30th with the same breeze we made two and one-half miles, nothing else to be noted, except that the saint's day of Quintano[a] was celebrated with the fine and spiritual wine of Malaga, kept in reserve from Spain for such occasions. This wine had attained at Cape Horn a degree of excellence which is unexplainable. The sun sets at 7:15 and the angelus took place at about 8.

The 31st, the wind freshened and the exercises of the cannon and the guns were continued.

On the 1st of June we continued with variable winds which made us tack every minute. We were looking at some light clouds. There was some heavy head swell, but regular. The pilot, Don Juan Maqueda,[17] says, speaking from his own experience, that without doubt farther on there are heavy seas which have been caused by some storm. Today we are in 38^0 latitude.[18]

June 2, we continue with the same wind, steering now to the west, now to the northeast, and occasionally to the northwest, with which we go a little faster, for we then make three miles; the weather somewhat squally and cloudy.

June 3, the same wind continues and the weather is worse, as every moment squalls blow which, although they worry the official who is on watch, soon pass away. Latitude 33^0 and some minutes. The experiments with the eudiometer continue and the cleaning between decks and that of the cabin, sweeping and scraping up the dirt that sticks to the floor, all with favorable results, very much to the satisfaction of our commander who gives the orders and to the doctor and his assistant, Don Tadeo,[19] who are very diligent in preventing any unfortunate casualty among our crew.

[a] Fernando Quintano, one of the officers.

June 4. It dawned very cloudy and quite cold and a very fresh wind continued which kicked up a very heavy swell. We went to tacking but gained little ground for the wind was almost ahead, which in technical terms is called a "short wind." It rained and all the portholes on the leeward side were closed, as the water could enter them, on account of the list of the ship. This operation is always practiced on such occasions, as well as that of covering with tarred strong linen the window in the quarter deck and which opens on the cabin. Chairs, tables, and other necessary utensils were strongly tied.

On the 5th the wind moderated a little in the morning but later it came back to blow strong again and it rained about 3 o'clock in the afternoon, leaving behind a calm, and a heavy sea, very regular. Latitude 34½°.

The 6th dawned with the weather serene and the wind short, steering towards the west; at night we sailed well. Latitude 35°.

The 7th, in the morning we had a fresh wind and from midday a calm until midnight, when the wind became fresh again and the sky overcast.

On the 8th the wind freshened, and was more quartering. At midday we were in 36° some minutes, the latitude of Monterey, distance from the coast 224 leagues.

The 9th, the same wind continued without change. A general clean-up was made and an experiment was made by the doctor on the air which is breathed in the whole ship. The result was satisfactory as all the endeavor of our commander is to prevent any pest, and up to the present time favorable results have been obtained by means of these continuous ship cleanings.

The 10th, the wind blew somewhat stronger, but at midday, we were becalmed although with a regular swell, so high that some very uncomfortable rolls were felt, and in one of these the foresail sheet went to pieces. Latitude 38° and some minutes.

On the 11th the calm continued and on this account the exercises with the cannon and the guns were repeated.

On the 12th the wind was stronger. At night, that is at the hour of the angelus, which was at 8 o'clock, we were going six miles, and at midnight, eleven miles, with much swell and heavy seas which made us close all the portholes and furl the gallant sails, leaving us only under the mainsail, maintopsail, the foresail, and the foretopsail. The ship rolled heavily from port to starboard.

31

The 13th, the wind increased still more and the main top gallant masts were taken down and reefs were taken in the topsail, the foresail, and the foretopsail. The meals were something to laugh about because the plates kept dancing about and everything else rolling around so that nobody could hold them.[20] We made three degrees of latitude to 41⁰.

The same wind continued although not so strong. The yards were put back in place, the portholes were opened, and the wind being more astern, we made two degrees from yesterday, being now in 43⁰. It rained a good deal and has done so every day since the 12th.

On the 15th the wind has been variable, but always fresh. We have made one degree, being in 44⁰.

The 16th, the favorable wind continues. It has rained since yesterday afternoon, but stopped at midday, at which hour we are in 45½⁰. At this latitude it is as cold as on the most severe day of a rigorous winter in Mexico, and here it is summer. It is 8 o'clock at night and the sun is setting. The rays shine straight through the porthole of my cabin and give me light to write at this hour.

The 17th, we continued with the wind astern in the direction of northeast, latitude 46⁰, the weather cloudy, dark and drizzling. Some ropes which were too old for the work have been replaced. The cold is increasing but with it comes the desire for eating and for drinking good wine. The common wine on board is of San Lucar.[21]

The 18th, the fog continues, although occasionally it clears up a bit so the sun can be seen. In the morning we had a calm with some rolls so heavy that at times the point of the lower studding sail boom touched the water. This always happens when there is a calm and a heavy regular sea, because as the ship cannot be steered without wind the waves move her and make her reel according to their course and direction. In the afternoon a breeze on the quarter blew and kept increasing so that we made two degrees of latitude during the afternoon and night, being then in 48⁰ of latitude.

On the 19th, the wind was variable, now from the south and now from the east. It finally became settled in the southwest. We are sailing six miles and it is cloudy. From the latitude of Monterey we have had more and more cloudiness every day. We are in 50⁰.

The 20th, we had the same variable winds but it became fixed in the southwest. In the afternoon the boat was put into the water and our commander with some officers went on board the *Atrevida*, which is to leeward, very near us for the last three days. It is quite marvelous that in this latitude the seas should be so moderate that the boat can be put in the water. We are in 52° latitude, in front of the Isla Carlotta,[a] but it cannot be seen as we are too distant from the coast. It is now 8:45 in the afternoon (because with the daylight we cannot call it night), the sun has just set and the angelus is after nine. Twilight continues until 10 and later, begins again at 2 in the morning and the sun rises at 2:30.

The 21st, day dawned very clear and cloudless and remained so until 5:30 in the afternoon when it clouded over. We had calm; we are in 53° some minutes, and the winds are variable.

The 22nd, the weather continues clear and the wind stronger. We have made one and a half degrees as we are now at 54° 30'.

The 23, a day memorable for the day and what occurred, namely the discovery off the bow to starboard at about 8:30 in the morning of the first land on the north coast. This land is a cape which extends far out to sea and which they call "Engaño."[b] The top of it is covered with snow. It looks like a great island but in the afternoon we found out it was an *ensenada* which this cape forms with the coast, a very extensive one which Quadra[22] called "Susto" on account of the many shoals which it contains.[c] In a little while all the coast showed up. It was about ten leagues in length, all of very broken and mountainous land, with some peaks and points very sharp and unequal whose summits were covered with snow, just like the mountain at the cape. Various ravines and declivities by the shape of the snow could be recognized. The geographer, Don Felipe Bauzá,[23] and the first pilot, Don Juan Maqueda, marked it and found it to lie in latitude 57°.[24] From here the coast begins to turn towards the west forming an extensive horseshoe which ends in Bering's Strait, where the last part of America ends, and Asia then continues. The geographer drew a view of the cape and I drew another. At night the cape was astern.

The 24th, the day dawned very fine and clear. We are in 58° latitude. We continued looking at the coast which is broken. The Punta del Cabo del Engaño[25] was covered with snow and the tops of the mountains on land all very rough and broken. Off the bow some very high mountains were seen, also all covered with snow. In the afternoon these were distant

[a] Queen Charlotte Islands.[26]

[b] Cape and Mt. Edgecumbe, so named by Captain Cook. Bodega had named the cape "Engaño" and the mountain "Jacinto" in 1775.

[c] I doubt this. Bodega himself gave no reason for naming the place "Susto." It was Sitka Sound.

eight leagues. The geographer marked them and drew a view of them and I drew another. During the night we had a wind from the south which carried us towards land and it was necessary to stand off to keep away from the coast.

On the 25th it dawned clear and we found we had doubled Cabo Buen Tiempo[a] (so it is called) but we had not gained anything because we were off it. We saw near at hand the mountains referred to. Allow me to give a description of them because to anyone not accustomed to see such a sight they are the greatest wonder.

A chain of mountains, with Mount Buen Tiempo, the highest and the greatest, hangs over the sea, forming an angle, all of a wonderful magnitude. It causes the greatest wonder and admiration to see them all covered with the purest snow from the foot to the summit, and the eyes do not get tired of looking at them. I placed myself on the poop in order to make a sketch of them but the frigid air which came off them made me stop very soon as I could not stand it. I went down to the quarter gallery on the port side and there without being so cold I drew a view, a great part of which the geographer adopted, adding it to the rest of the collection. Today we are in 58° 40'.

The 26th dawned cloudy and with the whole coast covered with clouds. We tacked several times as the winds were contrary for the direction in which we were proceeding. Today another range of mountains came in sight, more covered with grass and trees, but various streaks of snow on the side presented a pleasing view. Among them one streak which reaches down from the summit to the beach is very wide and ran in a wriggly manner. Between the geographer and myself we secured a good view of them.[27]

The 27th dawned cloudy and rainy. At 7 in the morning we found ourselves at the mouth of the bay of the Puerto de Mulgrave.[b] This port had a very wide entrance. On the port side the coast continues with a range of mountains, very steep and rough, and black from the foot halfway up. This with the contrast of the snow on the summits and some gorges above make a beautiful sight, although wild and uncommon. To enter the mouth we had to double a small point of low land all covered with snow. On the starboard side and in front of the coast are many

[a] Another name given by Cook. It is Fairweather in English.

[b] Discovered by La Pérouse but entered and named "Mulgrave" by George Dixon in 1787.[28]

islands and low rocks all densely forested with pine trees. From now on the cold began to bother us a great deal, so much so that we could hardly stand it, as there was so much snow on all sides and the fog was so thick that we could scarcely see the *Atrevida*, although she was quite close to us. When in the middle of this first small bay the geographer saw an opening which divided the range of mountains, forming a small strait. Within, a small *ensenada* presented itself to our view. Great was the joy of the commander and of all the officers because they believed, and with some foundation, that this might be the so much desired and sought-for strait, which would form a passage to the North Sea of Europe and which has cost so much trouble to all the nations in various expeditions which they have made for simply this end, and for the discovery of which a great reward has been offered. They now took out the manuscript of Ferrer Maldonado,[a] who marks this strait in the same latitude of 59° 30' of which we are talking and longitude [blank] and even the figures and the perspective agree with that which he gives. Ferrer Maldonado passed through a strait in the sixteenth century; I do not know in what year,[29] and had the glory of being the first and the last, as since then there has been no other, although it had been very frequently sought. According to his account we had on the starboard side the last point of America and on the port side the first of Asia. Transported with joy our commander steered towards the opening, sounding at each instant, but when near it forty fathoms were found, and he determined to anchor in the Puerto de Mulgrave, discovered in the year 1787 by Dixon,[30] and from there with the boats of the two corvettes, which are equipped, to reconnoiter this entrance and a great piece of coast which is to be explored before reaching the Puerto de Principe Guillermo, discovered by Captain Cook. With this thought we veered and doubled the point of the first island. We entered another small bay, and discovered the islands referred to which are numerous and very close together. We commenced to tack as the wind was ahead.

In a little while we saw coming towards us at great speed two canoes of Indians which shortly arrived alongside. The first view, when they were near, was one of great astonishment, both for the Indians and for us; for the Indians because they did not cease looking at the ships, although they advised us and we soon verified it, that these were not the first that they had seen; for us, because such strange and marvelous subjects presented

[a] See the writer's *Apocryphal Voyages* for an account of this man.

themselves to our sight.[a] They were dressed in skins of various colors, well-tanned, large and flexible. With one which hangs from a skin tied around their waist they cover their private parts and the other which reaches to the knees they hang from the shoulder like a cape. The skins seem to be of bears, tigers, lions,[b] and some of deerskins, and of marmots, with the hair outside. Their aspect would not be so disagreeable, although always wild, but the crude colors with which they paint themselves disfigure them entirely, as it seems that their idea of gala dress is to make themselves look as horrible as possible. Their hair is very thick and flaccid without any dressing or care, loose in the wayward natural manner, and covered with the greatest abundance of red ochre and grease, which according to the odor must be deer grease.[c] As soon as they were close to the ladder all except the steersman stood up, and at the sound of a stentorian and frightful voice which the ugliest one, who was in the center, uttered, they all extended their hands together in the form of a cross with great violence, and turning their heads to one side intoned a very sad song in their language, which, however, preserved tune and time. It was composed of only three notes although the measure varied. Soon they continued with other songs in this style, but very agreeable and sonorous.[d] Amid all that confusion the one in the middle could be heard dictating the words with a loud voice and carrying the measure, making various contortions and movements for this purpose, now to one side and now to the other, with his right arm extended and at times looking towards the sun. The others understood him perfectly, keeping good time. On other occasions, after a short pause, they continued with a great shout, repeating it three times, and, striking the palms of their hand against those who were carrying the tune and those of the rowers, finished by extending their arms in the form of the cross.

The corvettes continued tacking until they doubled the point of another island where the Puerto de Mulgrave opened.[31] Our commander then made signs to the Indians who had come aboard our ships to exchange sea-otter skins for beads which the corvettes brought for this purpose to go ashore. They understood the signal and went away, but they

[a] Yakutat Bay natives belong to the Tlingit linguistic family of the northwest coast, being the northernmost branch. Many early journals refer to the Tlingits as "Koluschaus" (with various spellings). N.

[b] There were no lions, possibly skins of the large Alaska brown bear were mistaken for lions. N.

[c] All the northwest coast tribes appear to have smeared their hair with grease and powdered it with red ochre and soot. N.

[d] We have many accounts of the natives greeting strangers with song. N.

did not stop for this reason following us all the afternoon, always singing songs which, although harsh on account of the pronunciation, were not very disagreeable. The king or chief went about directing his canoes in one made of skin, shaped like a weaver's shuttle with a deck of the same material in which there were two perfectly round holes by which they enter and leave, and which reach to their waist, where they tie them.[a] In these canoes they pass from one island to the other, and when there are bad storms and heavy seas they get inside them and leave them to the force of the waves, and are very secure as water does not enter anywhere. Finally at 7:30 in the afternoon we anchored in ten fathoms of water, about a pistol shot from the beach, and put out the small boats. This bay is very beautiful, all surrounded with various rocky islands, covered with big pine forests which present a beautiful view. I do not know its size but from what can be seen it seems to me it might be a little more or less than six leagues in circumference.

The 28th dawned with a very thick fog and very cold. Nevertheless our commander went on shore accompanied by various officers, soldiers, and armed sailors. The Indians made the sign of peace and sang so loudly that the shouting was heard on board. This day the place for taking water was found out from the cacique who pointed it out by signs, although we had some difficulty in understanding him. It is on a very pleasant island towards the east. The commander had various conferences with them, all amusing, which will be told when their character, dress, and religion are described.

The 29th, the fog cleared up somewhat and the observatory, a field tent,[32] was put ashore. The Indians continued to be very sociable and in return for clothes buttons, which they hang as pendants from their ears, gave us some rich, fresh salmon, at the rate of one for a button. This fish in the north is the most delicate thing which can be imagined. We could never satisfy ourselves with it notwithstanding that we ate an abundance of it. The chief, with his two sons, the eldest very ferocious and gigantic, asked the commander by signs to be allowed to come aboard. This the commander promised. He was entertained in the captain's cabin today. There was much to wonder at about these three men. The chief was an old, venerable and ferocious looking man with a very long gray beard, in a pyramidal form, his hair flaccid and loose on his shoulders. False hair over it in various locks, without any order or arrangement, made him look like

---

[a] About the southern limit of this type which is known as a "Kyak" among the Aleutians to the north and a "Bidarka" by the Russians. N.

a monster.[33] A large lion skin[a] for a cape was gathered in at the waist and left entirely bare his breast, arms, thighs, and endowments, very muscular and strong. All gave him a somewhat majestic air, which he manifested by speaking but little, measuredly, and with a sound which at times seemed to be the bellow of a bull. At other times it was softer and in speaking to his sons it was sweeter than in conversation. The elder of these was more than two yards tall, equally stout and muscular. He had his hair loose which, on account of its thickness, seemed like a horse's mane. It was very black like that of his beard. He was dressed in a black bear skin and very hairy, also in the form of a cloak which he fastened with some ornament, leaving bare at times all his nakedness, and passing to and fro over the quarterdeck, very proud and straight, his look full of ire, arrogant, and condescending. They both began to explain to us by signs that other ships had been there and that they had seen them. These we inferred were those of Dixon which were there in 1787. They also explained to us about some battle with very strange gestures and postures, which showed us they were very warlike. What we could draw from all their signs was that a short time before they had fought some other cacique who had killed the son of their chief. They showed us his helmet which was of a figure, and an extraordinary construction of wood, copper, and of straw cloth, and with a mask in front which appeared to be a wolf.[b]

From the 29th of June to July 2 little happened; only wood and water were taken and some skins were obtained in exchange at great cost as there were some of the crew who for a third of one skin dressed an Indian from head to foot. Today the boats left, well provided with arms, troops, and supplies for fifteen days. They went in search of the strait which I spoke of on the 27th of last month, and each one of our officers promised himself to find it, but they reckoned without their host. Our commander was in charge and in his longboat was Don Felipe Bauzá, the geographer, and in that of the *Atrevida* Don Antonio Tovar.[35] On the 3d, during the exchange of skins, some Indians on board stole some trifles and were made to produce them by the threat of punishment. This was told to the chief who regretted it very much, and gave his orders and in a little while they brought back what had been stolen. The result of this was some feeling which we noticed and we began to see them armed with bows and arrows, knives and lances. On a jacket and a cape belonging to a sailor being

---

[a] Possibly the skin of an Alaskan brown bear.

[b] A war helmet of wood, copper, and straw (straw—spruce root basketry—wolf carving, representing a leading crest of the Tlingit). N.[34]

stolen at the watering place, and on having seriously threatened the chief it was noted that they became irritated with us. A tree where we were taking wood fell close to one of them who became frightened and immediately laid hands on his knife, and all the others stood up in a state of preparedness. On account of my commission, and because the officers who accompanied me for the purpose of copying what was extraordinary and particular about their houses, had abandoned me, I saw myself in great peril in the house of the chief. I had scarcely commenced to work when with a great cry the cacique spoke to me in his language in an imperious tone and a threat that I should suspend my work. Engrossed in my work I paid little attention to him when the third time there was a grand chorus of shrieks by all the Indians. I came to myself and suspended my work which was well started. They caught hold of me and pushed me. I began to shout for my own people, but when I turned my face I did not see a single one. They formed a circle around me and danced around me knives in hand singing a frightful song, which seemed like the bellowing of bulls. In such circumstances I resolved to carry out their mood and I began to dance with them. They let out a shout and made me sit down, and by force made me sing their songs which according to the gestures which they made I understood as ridiculing me. In such a situation I feigned ignorance and shouted louder making the same contortions and gestures. They were very much pleased at this and I was able with my industry to gain their good will with a figure which I sketched for them with a coat etc., and dressed like ourselves. They marveled very much at this and began pointing at it with a finger exclaiming "Ankau!" "Ankau!" which is to say "Señor", and as they call their chief. So they quieted down and insisted on giving me fish to eat. I excused myself as much as I could but seeing that they threatened me I had to eat. Soon they offered me some women, pointing out some and reserving for me some others. Seeing that I did not move they then made signs to me with their hands that they were giving them to me so I might violate them. At this moment a sailor arrived who was looking for me as the boat was going aboard. I complained to some of the officers that they had abandoned me and they excused themselves by telling me that the natives who had remained on the beach were peaceable and therefore they had inferred that they would not do me any harm. I forgot to say that as soon as they saw the sailor, they believed that more were coming and I took occasion of the opportunity to get away.[36]

On the 4th the two corvettes continued taking wood and an Indian threatened to strike Don José Bustamante. This had the effect of our again distrusting them and they us, because they were aggrieved when by way of punishment the trade in skins on board was suspended, and because they have always seen the officers of the *Atrevida* with their commander well armed, and ourselves as well because we considered the unfortunate consequences which might happen to us if these natives molested us, who like warriors at the least thing became angry. At 5 in the afternoon the two longboats were seen doubling the point of a small rocky island and entering this bay. They were rowing and sailing. They arrived and the commander and the geographer told us that at about twelve on the 2d they found themselves at the mouth of the strait. The tide was against them and so they waited to enter it and anchored until the next day. On the 3d they entered and found all their hopes frustrated, because what they believed to be a strait was a port entirely closed on all sides by very steep high mountains. Nevertheless they did all they could and stayed there all day tacking, eluding the many fields of ice which they could see came down by the gullies on the mountain making such an echo that at first they thought it was an earthquake. As they went on they found greater difficulty to pass, for the fields of ice which surrounded them on all sides were more numerous. They saw from the middle of this great bay, which was as far as they could reach, that the other half was entirely frozen so that one could pass up to the wall of the mountains with dry feet if it were not for the risk that he would be crushed, as they had seen happen with some pieces which were floating about and which had been so crushed when they fell into the water. They came close to the bank and anchored. From here the geographer drew some different views and the commander wrote on a paper the following: "In the year 1791 the longboats of his Majesty's *Descubierta* and *Atrevida* discovered this port which they named 'Desengaño' and 'Bahia de las Bancas'."[37] They put this paper in a bottle and closed it very tight with sealing wax. The sailors made a deep hole and buried the bottle under a hard stone, surrounding it with rocks and soil. While they were conducting this operation they missed a sailor, and in searching for him they had to waste all afternoon until they saw him coming, almost dead with cold and totally changed. It happened that on seeing the commander's zeal and desire to find the strait he went on foot above Frozen Bay to satisfy himself by his own eyes where was the end of the bay. He actually reached the farthest point and saw that it ended in a copious river which ran between those mountains and was lost to view.

winding about like a snake. We missed him at midday and he came about 10 o'clock in the afternoon (I call it so because there is no night). According to his account it was a miracle that he had escaped with his life, not only because of the cold but because from one side to the other the sea submerged it and then it froze over again.[38] In view of this feat it will not be thought strange to say that the Spaniards undertake the most arduous enterprises, risking their lives for the honor of their country. It is worth recording his name, José Berelo,[a] a native of Coruña in the kingdom of Galicia, twenty-eight years of age, of medium though sturdy stature.

The 5th dawned cloudy and cold. The official, Don Juan Bernaci,[39] made a signal from land at the beginning of day that he was preparing the observatory to take aboard. We thought that he was asking assistance from the Indians who had been insolent. Our commander at once gave an order to arm the men and make ready the cannon. He went ashore with Don Cayetano Valdés and they arrived when the Indians had formed a party and setting at nought their lives, with their knives in their hands, they came to the muzzle of the gun. Don José Bustamante, to see if they could be frightened, fired a cannon shot and at once they covered themselves with their skins and others looked about to see who had fallen. This made them more insolent still, but the chief and his son were by a coincidence on board the *Atrevida*. Bustamante seized them when he saw that our people were in a fight, and threatened to punish them if he did not order his Indians to keep quiet. This had the desired effect as with great shouts from on board he commenced to hold back his men who were uneasy and very anxious to come to blows with our people. In spite of the voice of the chief whom they saw a prisoner, they came very near to attacking us, having collected a considerable body of the Indians of this island. One of them scarcely saw the movement than he ran along the beach and put himself in front of them with his dagger, attacking Don Juan Bernaci and the whole body of our people. It would have been very easy to finish off all of them with such advantageous arms as guns and pistols which they had in their faces while defending the embarkation of the rest and fronting the enemy. The chief believed we were angered about some goats which an Indian had stolen and which he ordered him to bring. It was something to laugh at to see him in his canoe giving the sign of peace while hoisting high his goats after Bustamante had turned him loose.[40] Our ships answered with the signal of peace and they then asked to come back for the trade in skins. As soon as this was conceded they laid

[a] The Malaspina account gives him a different name.[41]

41

aside all their fierceness and came alongside very contented in their canoes as if nothing had happened. This afternoon the kedges were raised leaving the vessel over the anchor which we weighed at 6 in the afternoon and made sail for the Puerto del Principe Guillermo. When only a pistol shot from the port side of the channel we struck at the bow in two fathoms of water between some rocks. The confusion which such an unexpected accident caused was great but by means of a kedge anchor which was stretched from the stern, the longboat of the *Atrevida* and our boats, which towed us for more than an hour, our Maria Santissima was pleased that we should get off, remaining moored by the kedge anchor until morning, when at 3:30 we again made sail, not without great difficulty in getting in the kedge anchor, which held so fast that in spite of the capstan it would not give way.

On the 6th we continued with a fresh wind in view of the coast which we lost sight of in the afternoon when the wind strengthened.

On the 7th on account of having tacked during the night we were at daybreak in front of the coast to the west of Puerto de Mulgrave. This coast is very high; the great mountain of San Elias can be seen and all the mountains are covered with snow, everything except the lowlands at the shoreline.

I proposed to give a description of the Indians at Puerto de Mulgrave; this I shall now do with the greatest brevity possible. In the first place they are of medium stature but robust and strong. Their physiognomy has some resemblance to that of all Indians, except that their eyes are very far apart and are long and full. The face is more round than long, although from the cheeks, which are very bulging, to the chin it is somewhat more pointed. Their eyes are sparkling and alive, although always manifesting a wild and untamed air, a consequence of the methods by which they are brought up. They have little beard although there is no general rule about this as I have seen some with a very full one. This and the hair of their head is so thick that is looks like the mane of a horse. The women have the same facial characteristics and if it was not for the red ochre and black soot which they put on some of them would not be very ugly although in general I would not venture to say that they were good looking.

All of them, men and women, generally speaking, have something of Chinese features. Their dwellings or habitations are very poor. Here can be seen their disorderly filth, for they are more like pigsties than the habitations of human beings. This causes such a fetid and disagreeable odor on their belongings and persons that you cannot stand it. The houses

e on the bank of the sea at the point which the channel for leaving the
rt forms. They are of board placed over the trunk of a tree without any
der. This traverses it and forms the ridge pole on which the boards rest
one side and the other,[a] the tree trunk being held up by others,
rpendicular ones, sunk in the ground. On the top of the roof all their
longings can be seen, canoes made, others in skeleton, skins half-cured,
od, and other various rubbish. Inside you see the same. What cannot
put outside is put inside. Here you can see some square wooden boxes.[b]
l their ornament is reduced to a mask on the four fronts with the mouth
en, badly carved with the teeth inverted and in others by way of
nament they have them placed in a parallel line. In another place you
n see a great quantity of fish, which seemed to us like our conger eel,[c]
ring at the fire, and hanging from some sticks. In the same way they
at their salmon. Many skins are hung about, bows here, arrows there,
ives, cuirasses, bundles of clothes; many children, all naked, and some
en, other suckling children in their cradles, the women at their work, so
at everything appears in the greatest confusion. They are always eating
d heating themselves at the fire in the middle of the hut. Their
stenance and daily meal is as follows: They catch a fish and pass a stick
rough it from the tail to the mouth which they fasten in the ground.[d]
ey keep turning it towards the fire. As soon as it is softened they place it
a straw basket[e] which is very flexible and is so closely woven that not a
op of water can come out. In this they put it to cook with seawater, and
that the basket may not burn underneath they have various red hot
nes which they throw inside, according as necessity demands, always
intaining the heat until the dried fish in small fragments forms a mess[f]
d then they eat it with some long deep spoons made of horn.[g] I do not
ow to what animal the horn belongs because there are no bulls, cows,
rses, burros, mares, or other animals among the Indians nor do they
ow of them. When the Indians are newly born they put them in a cradle
de of a kind of reed very well worked. Two skins hang down from each

able type plank houses. They were of poor construction on account of the lack of suitable building
aterials. N.

type of general purpose box common among the Tlingit, Haida, and Tsimshian, though the majority
ly had painted totemic design on the front and back. N.

annot identify it. They should have had supplies of halibut and perhaps "black cod." N.

sh cooking by passing a stick through it lengthwise was practiced by all the coast Indians. N.

his will be a specimen of the famous Tlingit spruce root basket—a type of which the Yakutats made the
est examples.

t stone cooking—a similar method used all along the coast. N.

ountain sheep horn. N.

side of this which they fold over the breast of the baby and which covers it down to the knees. These are joined by a skin which through various holes extends from one side to the other. The creatures are dressed with their arms inside, all with skins, and thus they put them inside the cradle, and cover them very well down to the feet as stated. Thus they manage the affair, giving them to suck and leaving them stretched out on the ground.[a] As soon as they are born they pass a very delicate feather through the cartilege of the nose for the purpose of making a hole in it, and in consequence the hole gets bigger so that when they are grown up they can put a nail of considerable size through it as they do, as they all have holes in their noses.[b] The women in addition to the hole in their nose make one in their lower lip horizontally in which they place a roll of wood of elliptical form, hollowed out on one side and the other, and thick enough to hold it between the teeth and the lip.[c] The size of it appears incredible as well as the custom of wearing it. Clasping this roll with the lip they talk, eat, and do everything. We do not know if this is distinctive of the married women, although to me it seems so, because I have not noted it in other than these, and the unmarried ones do not use it.[d] All of them tattoo their arms and hands in lines of various design and so remain forever.[e] The dress of the women is very modest. It consists of a robe of tanned skin and without hair which covers them from their throat down to their feet, and the breast and arms, down to the wrist. There is a sleeve which is wide but modest.[f] In all, this tunic has the same form as that which they put on the effigy of Jesus Nazareno and tie around the waist. Besides this robe they wear a cape or square cape also of skin which is held on the right shoulder by a piece of leather and some living on the banks of the sea wear [only] a fringe. Some use these cloaks made strictly of marten skins.

The dress of the men is as I have stated, of various skins, the most ordinary being of black bear, and very hairy. When it rains and they have no hats they cover their heads with the same skin of the head of a bear,

[a] The cradle is well described, but I have not seen a Tlingit cradle. N.

[b] Nose piercing was practiced among all the coast tribes. N.

[c] Labrets in the lower lip of women were noted by explorers and traders as in use from Queen Charlotte Sound (Bella Bella Kwakiutl) to northern limits of Tlingit Territory. Though later the authorities have stated this custom was not practiced by the Yakutats. N.

[d] The young woman of "rank" secured her first labret when "coming of age" and many were married at this time. The women without labrets, probably of "poor" families or possibly slaves. N.

[e] The Tlingit according to more recent observations did not tattoo to the same extent as the Haida of Queen Charlotte Islands—where totemic designs were worked on many parts of the body. For "line" tattooing references will be found for many tribes of the Pacific Coast. N.

[f] Early accounts of these Indians on the Northwest Coast in many instances state the women were more modest than the men in the way of dress. N.

which makes them look like some Hercules. The rest of the skin they gather in at the waist by means of a piece of leather and what is left of the animal, claws and tail, etc., hangs down to the middle of the leg. From this may be inferred that the arms, breast, stomach and belly are uncovered except the shoulders and the rump. In order that this skin may not get loose, they sustain it on the right shoulder by means of another connecting piece of leather. Some besides this wear another skin which we can call a cape or cloak, as it serves the same purpose. Others go entirely naked with a breech clout. Their hair is loose (among the women also) but groomed with more care on one side than the other, leaving the parting of the hair uncovered, covered with red ochre, and their faces painted with it which makes them look horrible.[a] The fighting Indians wear all their arms, a breast-plate, back armor, a helmet with a visor or at least what serves that purpose. The breast and back armor are a kind of coat of mail of boards two fingers thick, joined by a thick cord which after being *berbirlis* by *as* and *embes* with much union and equality joins them. In this junction the thread takes an opposite direction, it being the case that even here the arrows cannot pass through, much less in the thickest part of the boards. This breast plate is bound to the body by the back. They wear an apron or armor from the waist to the knees of the same character which must hinder their walking.[b] Of the same material they cover the arm from the shoulder to the elbow, on the legs they use some leggings which reach to the middle of the thigh, the hair inside. They construct the helmet of various shapes; usually it is a piece of wood, very solid and thick, so much so, that when I put on one it weighed the same as if it had been of iron. They always have a great figure in front, a young eagle or a kind of parrot, and to cover the face they lower from the helmet a piece of wood which surrounds this and hangs from some pieces of leather in the middle of the head to unite with another one which comes up from the chin. They join at the nose, leaving the junction for the place through which to see.[c] It is to be noted that before they put this armor on they put on a robe like that of the women but heavier and thicker, and with certain kinds of work.

[a] According to Niblack the facial painting of the Tlingit took the place of tattooing as practiced by the Haida. N.

[b] The Tlingit manufactured the most elaborate armor of the coast tribes. Those farther south relied on hand-tanned hides to a great extent. Lisiansky gives a good illustration of the various sections described by Suría and Niblack gives details of the manufacture. Walter Hough in the *Report of the National Museum*, Washington, for 1893 (p. 637), states that there are four sets of armor collected by Malaspina in 1791 in the Musco Arqueologico, Madrid. He questions the collecting locality but I would certainly say Yakutat Bay. N.[42]

[c] Helmets of heavy wood construction carved to represent a "crest" of the owner have also been collected from the Haida and Tsimshian. N.

They hang *catucas* and the bow they put over the arm to which it hangs back of the shoulders. They clasp a short lance, a knife, and a hatchet. Such is the equipment of a warrior. The lance is a heavy stick of black wood,[a] very well worked, and at the point they tie on the blade of a great knife which they obtain from Englishmen in exchange for their skins. The knife which they carry in their belt is the same as ours for the same reason. The hatchet is a black stone of the size, figure, and edge of our iron hatchet.[b] They fasten it to a heavy stick and make use of it in war and in their other necessities. The bows and arrows are the same as those of all other Indians.[c] All this I know because an Indian who armed himself for us to see it, pointed it all out to us by signs.

Their household furniture is little. For their children they make some toys with heads of marble for them to play with.[d] They gamble with some little sticks, about eight or nine fingers long, and a finger in thickness, very well made. They count up to fifty with various signs, which differ one from the other. They shuffle them and then stretch one or two on the ground. From what we could make out the companion must pick out from these two the one which has been hidden by the one doing the shuffling, which he recognizes by signs. If he succeeds the little sticks pass to his companion and if not the same man continues the same shuffling.[e] There is sufficient reason for thinking that with this game they put up their persons and whoever loses has to be at the disposition of the other, because one of our sailors went to play with one of them, and having lost as usual, because he did not know the game, the Indian became very contented and made a sign to the sailor to embark in his canoe, because he was now his, and on being resisted the Indian insisted, indicating by signs that he had won. The pots and jars in which they cook are those already referred to.

[a] Western yew. N.

[b] The hatchet described by Suría is probably what is known in more recent works as the "long-handled" adze"; it was mounted like the shipwright's adze and was the general purpose tool of the northern coast Indians. N.

[c] On closer examination they would have been found to incorporate certain features peculiar to the Yakutat, adopted to meet the particular hunting problems of their district. N.

[d] Something similar was noted in the Haida canoes by Father Crespi of Juan Pérez's expedition, when off Lángara Island, Queen Charlotte Islands. (See H.E. Bolton's translation, University of California Press, 1927, page 333). N.

[e] Dixon also saw the game played at Port Mulgrave. La Pérouse and Kotzebue also mention it. The sticks are from four to five inches long and vary in thickness from that of the average pencil to the average little finger. The number of sticks in a bundle appears to have been immaterial, anywhere from 20 to 70. I have collected a very fine set from the Haida with the latter number. It is a guessing game to locate certain "marked" sticks in the bundle. Kotzebue says "they lose all their possessions at this game, even wives and children." N.

Their food consists of fish: salmon, smelts,[a] and another which looks like a conger eel.

We could not find any trace of their religion although to me it appears that they bestow some worship on the sun.[b] I am of this opinion because in order for the chief to make us understand that our commander was taking observations on shore, he told us that *Ankau* (which is the same as Señor), our commander, was looking at *Ankau*. Therefore if this word means a superior, as so they name their chiefs, and the same word is used to speak of the sun, it seems possible that they are rendering it adoration. In their burials they keep some system and put up monuments to the posterity of the good memory of their dead. The geographer gave us an account of the various monuments which he had seen on the bank of a river by which he had entered to take a certain bearing, a river which was quite close to the anchorage. One morning the commander arranged for us to go in the boat to look at these monuments which no voyager had seen.[43] We therefore went and saw their sepulchres in this form. A little bit away from the bank of the river, or rather arm of the sea (because this enters into it and by signs the Indians even gave us to understand that it divided the island and passed to the other side of the great sea), there is some undergrowth very fruitful in wild celery, camomile, like that in Spain, and many other herbs which I do not know, besides a great abundance of strawberries, so many in fact, that those who went were able to satisfy themselves, and many pine trees. Near these on the right-hand side there were two square boxes raised from the soil 2½ yards and held up by four pillars, also square. Of these boxes that on the left-hand side had on the face of it to the front various masks and other signs of which we do not know the significance. At the foot of the boxes, that is, on the surface of the ground there are others, which were those that we explored and inside we found a calcined skeleton between some mats. This box with all it contained we took on board. Farther on along the same beach there is a skeleton house which is reduced to three frames, each one of three sticks placed parallel to each other at a proportionate distance, the one in the middle being higher than the other two.[c] On the base of the poles which face inside there are various designs. The chief whom we found there

[a] The "smelts" notes were far more likely to have been "herring" or "culachon," the latter being the great oil fish of the coast tribes. N.

[b] I can find little in the literature available to show that the sun is a prominent character in their myths and legends. N.

[c] George Dixon also describes burials at Yakutat. Possibly the three "sticks" at the "skeleton house" were for supporting the boxes containing the heads, as stated by Dixon. N.[44]

made various signs to us which nobody could understand, but what we thought was that either before or after the funeral ceremonies they have a dance in this place, which must be of some particular significance, as after pointing out that they covered these poles with something he took out his knife and stuck it into the stick and at once began to dance with a very happy gesture, making various movements and emitting an "O" with his throat. Some were of the opinion that it might be that after some important victory against their enemies they celebrated in this place and they founded this opinion on his action in sticking in the knife. We noted that whenever some canoe from the neighborhood whose Indians are subject to some other chief come to this island they make a salute to it which is worth describing. As soon as they see them they go down to the beach and all together in unison kneel until they remain on their knees and on standing up they utter a great cry, very ugly, and ferocious, on a *gangora* which sounds something like an N. This they repeat three times and at the last end with a very sharp and quavering shriek. On the occasion of receiving foreigners they make use of many songs all different, as I have described on the 27th when we entered this port. They also make use of others of this style in order to ask for peace as we found out as the result of having suspended commerce with skins with them for a day. Believing that we were very angry they did not stop singing all afternoon and night and as this song is interesting, I find it necessary to give an account of it.

They divided themselves into three parties each of considerable numbers and planted themselves on the beach in front of the ships. At the end of each song they finished with a kind of laugh which jointly and in measure they sustained on this sound, Xa Xa Xa Xa Xa. In others they ended with another sound which cannot be described but it was like the barking of a dog. Thus they went on all night, leaving us unable to sleep.

Their language is very harsh. It abounds greatly in KK's and HH's. On board there are some who assert that it seems to be the tone of a monarch shouting wildly and in an arrogant and fearful tone. A curious man on board had the patience to put down some words but he did not keep on because he thought it was impossible to transfer to paper such combinations of letters, some of which are impossible, such as bg. An enemy they call *cuteg*, which they pronounce like one who is clearing his throat of phlegm. I have made out the following: *ankaiui* means Señor or superior; *chouut* means woman; *kuacan*, a friend; *tukriunegui* means a child at the breast; and *anegti*, a boy.[a]

They use canoes of different sizes. Ths ordinary ones are ot wood shaped like a weaver's shuttle and of this figure.[b] [Figure] Others are of skin sewed to a framework of poles well constructed and tied, and are like this.[c] [Figure] The two holes in the center are for entering. Half the body from the waist down is inside and they seat themselves on their heels as is their ordinary custom, and thus they manage the canoe with the oars. They use no rudder and in order to keep going straight they paddle the same number of times first on one side and then on the other with great speed. Their oars are very curious and are painted like the canoes with various marks and masks. They have some leather thongs which pass through the entire deck of the canoe and are tied on the sides. These are like stay rods where they put their lances and arrows and their oars when they are moving along. [Some later-written, almost undecipherable notes] [Then follow seven sketches].

The 8th, we lost sight of the coast because the northwest wind had arisen and was quite fresh. The sky was obscured and hazy.

The 9th, we continued with the same wind but the horizon was somewhat clearer.

The 10th, the wind strengthened and we began to feel much cold weather, the sky misty and hazy, and some swell.

The 11th, the wind shifted a little to the east clearing away the fog.

The 12th, the wind died down somewhat and gave an opportunity to make an observation. The *Atrevida* was spoken so that she could be advised of the results of the observation. We caught a porpoise which Mr. Haenke says is called *carpintero*[d] and on my telling him that those which I had seen were not like it he satisfied me by saying that those in the latitudes of the Far North such as that where we were now speaking, were entirely distinct.

[a] Of the six words recorded by Suria a modern rendering can be found for the following (but taken from tribes farther south):
    ankaiui chief ankao — in Sitka dialect by Dall
    Ankau
    chouut woman shawut — by Gibbs
    Kuacan friend heha-kaua — by Gibbs
    Tukriunegui child at breast te-kwun-neh-yeh (infant) — by Gibbs
    Where I have been able to find Yakutat words in modern vocabularies for the above of Suria's there is nothing one can recognize other than "Shawut." N.[45]

[b] This refers to the dugout. On page 248 the same expression is used for the skin canoes. N.

[c] The Kyak of the Aleutians, a two-man "bidarka" of the Russians. The dugout of the Yakutats followed the same general lines of the well known northern (or Haida) canoe but had a peculiar bow somewhat "crescent shaped." N.

[d] A species of this district is Phoceonoides dalli (True) Dalls Purpoise. N.

The 13th dawned quite cloudy, but at ten it cleared up a little and we discovered to the west the coast and some islands which the pilots said were Amia but I did not think this was true.[46] We stood off from the land at 5 o'clock in the afternoon and soon lost sight of them. The pilots marked them and found [six more sketches] in what direction they bore. I do not put it down here on account of this note.

Being desirous of writing down an individual account of all the incidents of this voyage in technicological nautical terms, as they are so fruitful and interesting, principally in matters of geography, and deal with the navigation of the northwest coast of America, and in view of the fact that few come to these parts, I proposed to myself on my departure from Acapulco to keep a diary with the greatest formality. I considered that the execution of this would be more easy because our commander had allotted to the second pilot and myself a cabin. I do not wish to treat of the inconvenience because this is not the place to speak of it. I will only say that stretched in my bed my feet were against the side of the ship and my head against the bulkhead, which is what they call the timbers which inclose the cabin. From my breast to the deck, which was my roof, the distance is only three inches. This confined position does not allow me to move in my bed and I am forced to make for myself a roll of cloth to cover my head, although this suffocates me, but this is a lesser evil than being attacked by thousands of cockroaches, which are such a great pest that you see some individuals with sores on their foreheads and bites on their fingers.

This situation brought about my asking questions of the pilot about such doubts as occurred to me. I noted that he was slow in answering and vague in explaining the matters about which I asked him, always leaving me in doubt. I therefore begged him to lend me his journal so I could keep in touch with what was most worth noting down, and also because I have much to do and have not the smallest place for writing the events day by day, unless I take some inopportune moment. To this he answered that he could not comply with my request by reason of the special orders of the Minister of Marine[47] who did not wish the least notice of the voyage to be divulged until the Minister himself should publish it fully corrected. Although I told him that I would not furnish the least copy he refused me absolutely. I made the same request of the first pilot's apprentices, with the same result. For this reason my journal does not proceed with all the

a What he means by this I do not know.

exactness possible in the realm of geography.[a] Nevertheless, I will endeavor to gain information with sagacity and astuteness. At the same time I shall omit what I know to be useless and what only interests the pilots. I do not do this with the information regarding the Indians as these are more interesting generally and I have endeavored to observe all their actions and movements and as this is so much a part of my business it is easier for me to gain the information than for the others. To this may be added my understanding the character of the Indians through a period of thirteen years' residence in Mexico. This gives me an opportunity to make my combinations by comparing these with the others. In truth my opinion is very far distant from that of those who are writing for the work.[b] In this a sublime idea is set forth as different as possible from what is seen by the eyes of whomever beholds it. In this he will encounter a pleasure which he did not have on looking at it. Enough of digression.

On the 10th the wind shifted more to the southeast bringing on much fog and at times fine rain. We bore towards land and at 8 in the morning discovered it to windward. As we had the wind ahead we went on tacking and marking and reconnoitering the coast. At 10 it cleared up and we saw we were very close to Cabo Hinchinbrook at the entrance to Principe Guillermo.[c] It is a mountainous country covered with pine trees. The rock of the mountains is very black, forming certain crosswise bands in great promontories, and the tops are covered with much snow. We drew very close to the coast for it is very steep. We were so close to it, in fact, at a distance of about a league, that no bottom was to be found with a line of 100 fathoms, that is, 600 feet. While doubling the point of Cabo Hinchinbrook the wind strengthened so that we furled the mainsail and topgallant sails, taking reefs in the maintopsail, the foresail, and the foretopsail. We approached the coast and at 12 were in the channel between the Isla Montague and the Isla Magdalena, the last to windward and the other to leeward. We also doubled another island which was in the middle of the channel and which cost us much trouble to pass on account of the force of the wind, which was from the bow.[d] The anchors being ready the boat was launched and Don Juan Sánchez[48] embarked in it charged with sounding and hunting for a good anchorage in the Puerto de Santiago,[e] on the Isla de Magdalena, the mouth of which we were now about to enter.

[a] In spite of this statement he copied from some one's log which was used in the printed account of the expedition.
[b] He means the ambitious grandiose work of Malaspina.
[c] Prince William Sound.
[d] Seal Rocks, the Isla Triste of the Spaniards.
[e] Port Etches.

We continued tacking, when some gusts of wind blew so strong through the openings in the mountains that it cost us some labor to keep on our feet. In one of these the yard of the topgallantsail at the bow split in half and this caused some disorder and confusion as the wind was now very strong, and we were embayed on a lee shore at the entrance, very close to the coast and with danger on all sides. The sounding was continued and 60, 70, and 80 fathoms were found, the only thing to console us. Our commander, seeing that we were so embayed, that it was 2:30 in the afternoon and that we could not enter without danger with that wind and sea, which was very heavy, resolved to sheer off and content himself with having reached the entrance of Principe Guillermo and thus exceeded the orders of the court which had commanded him to go up to 60° latitude. Here we were in 61° and some minutes, the season was advanced and he considered that we should prepare for our return to Acapulco. In effect we stood off, and the wind changed to the southeast with the same force. Although in these parts this wind is very dirty it suddenly abated, leaving as clear and beautiful a day as I have ever seen in my life. On coming in we had a northwest wind off the prow and when we found it necessary to turn back it changed to the southeast so that we were in desperation. The boat with the pilot, Don Juan Sánchez, which had gone to hunt for a good anchorage in the Puerto de Santiago, in the Isla Magdalena, came back. With this on board we encountered another difficulty which was to double a small rocky island in the middle of the channel. Our commander issued orders to stand off to sea by tacking.

All day we were working to get out and although we were afraid that we could not succeed in view of the strong wind, the heavy seas, and the tide which was entering and carrying us on the rocks, the efforts of our excellent seamen who labored this day excellently well, together with the fact that our corvettes answered the helm, was sufficient to enable us to save ourselves by tacking in the channel and in keeping away from the coast. About 5 in the afternoon the great Ensenada de Principe Guillermo could be seen where there are many great mountains. [This last page is so written over later that it is impossible to make it all out. It can be seen, however, that he speaks of a canoe with two Indians coming near.] A little later about 6 in the afternoon two other large canoes could be seen and a greater number of Indians who were armed with bows and lances held on the canoes by means of the thongs which passed through them. They made the greatest effort to approach us but they also were unable to succeed, but they did get alongside of the *Atrevida*. We went on tacking in order to pass the rocky island but about 11:30 when the sun had already set the commander decided to take the island to leeward and to proceed to the open sea between it and the Isla Montague. This was the longest day that we encountered in this latitude and there would have been more to admire if the great darkness which we principally found in the morning had not prevented as I have just said.

Finally we passed to the west of the Isla Triste. There was no reef while those which extended to the east of it and which we could not pass had no less extension than a short half-mile. At midnight we were already free from danger, without having found bottom at 2 miles distant with some thirty fathoms of line. We luffed towards the southeast and forced sail in order to get away somewhat from the Isla Montague.

The 11th, our navigators have seen in this neighborhood some small islands called Hijosa,[a] so-named in honor of the Comissario de Marina who at present is living in the Department of San Blas, namely Don Francisco Hijosa. Neither Captain Cook nor Captain Dixon have included it in their maps, an omission which can not be understood. The first had gone out to the west of the Isla Montague, but there is no excuse for the second because his course during the first year took him by that immediate vicinity, and because he found fault with very little decorum with our old navigators about some errors in their hydrography on the innumerable coasts which they had explored. Regardless of this the tacks which were necessary to us show its actual position, and the weather which had now settled in the east and was at the same time overcast and tempestuous might have caused us to make an error which might have produced most unfortunate consequences because it was natural to stand to the second quarter not only in order to get away from the Isla Montague but also to reach anew the meridian at which we should begin our explorations. In effect a little after the setting of the sun the weather had become overcast to an extraordinary degree, the sea had risen, and the wind freshened to such an extent that we could not stand under the maintopsail reefed. We had to look after the repair of the foresailyard whose bolt rope had been broken the previous afternoon. With this object another foresail was substituted while the other was being repaired. Our course was to the south. We very soon lost sight of land on account of the fog, neither the sea going

[a] Middleton Island.

down, nor the wind nor the rain ceasing. At midday we tacked around on the four principal winds with reefs in the maintopsails, considering ourselves to be in the latitude of 59° 30'.

Shortly the wind died away and was succeeded by light breezes but without varying its direction. Some of the fog was dissipated so that at 2 o'clock in the afternoon we were able to see off the beam on the starboard side at a distance of 3 leagues a flat island which we at once knew to be Hijosa, although its position in latitude and longitude were quite different and it seemed to be only a single island. The calm lasted but a short time. At 7 in the afternoon the wind was again fresh from the first quarter and was accompanied with much rain. Although this did not stop we were soon in a calm, having enjoyed the advantage for some time of winds from the second quarter. Finally at daybreak the fog cleared away and the sea fell considerably. Our navigation since the preceding afternoon had had but a single object, namely to keep to the south of the island which we had sighted.

The already hinted necessity of directing our course to Acapulco for the reasons that the season was very much advanced and it was necessary to reconnoiter the great piece of coast from Cabo Hinchinbrook to the Cabo and Monte Buen Tiempo, a reconnaissance which was indispensable not only to dispel once for all the scrupulous doubts which might remain about the desired passage to the Atlantic of Europe but because this was a piece of coast which, except the great mountain of San Elias, marked and situated by Captain Cook, is not known to have been seen by any traveler, a mountain elevated above the level of the sea to a very considerable height and visible with clear weather twenty leagues out to sea. These justifiable considerations deprived us in part of the glory of following the route projected of going up to 70° and 80° where the Glacial Sea and the South Sea[49] unite by the Strait of Bering, and carry out the same explorations as the immortal Cook. This created the greatest desires of our commander and the officers of both corvettes to find ourselves in such a favorable position, that is simply following the course to the southwest, leaving to starboard Cook's River and falling down exploring the coast until the point of the Isla de Onalaska,[50] which was between 50° and 52° was doubled, and then going up to the latitude referred to and exploring also the coast of Asia, which in this region trends towards the north. Between this coast and the last part of America is found the true and indicated Strait of Bering where ends this considerable part of the world. This is not traversable as these seas are constantly frozen, although various nations have entered it. Spain does not take second place to any nation in heroism as it has always shown during all the centuries, whenever she sends out subjects of known valor and prudence such as our actual commander. On this occasion this was particularly noticeable, for even the humblest sailors formed bands which murmured about the plans taken of reconnoitering the coast because they were ignorant of the real motives which, with the accord of the officers, had been reached in the cabin. They believed that what was a wise precaution was a lack of spirit and their disgust and impatience were notable because they came to comprehend that the English had the advantage of us in these discoveries. Our commander, far from being disquieted by such demonstrations of the natural and inveterate spirit of heroism of our nation, gave as an example an invitation to a celebration in the cabin in view of the officers, thus prudently cutting short such rumors.

It remains to be stated that on the morning of the 12th, the weather being clear and favorable a skin canoe like those at the Puerto de Mulgrave came out from the Isla Hijosa with two Indians in their respective holes and with their arrows and lances tied on the deck of the canoe by way of precaution. Notwithstanding the advantage in sailing of our ships they rowed with such spirit and swiftness that in a short time they were at our stern close to the rudder. We repeatedly entreated them to come on board but they excused themselves as being timid and gave the well-known signs of friendship by stretching out their arms and repeating this word *La li, La li!* which is equivalent to *koacan* or friend. At the same time they manifested to us their desires for us to come to anchor in a port which according to their signs lay on the west side of the island. Having lost hope of this they departed. The dress which the natives in Montague wear consists of sea-otter skins, a blouse of flexible and transparent gut, the folds of which are fastened around the hole in the canoe. Their hats are like Chinese hats, their hair is loose, covered with red ochre, their ears and nose are bored and hanging from these are some long narrow leather thongs like tape, while passing through the nose is a tooth or bone of some land animal.

The weather now being serene we continued on our course, as the weather permitted, at times in sight of the coast and at other times not, marking the principal points with the greatest exactitude in order to construct the geographical maps, the principal object of this scientific expedition. Captain Cook holds a point of land which extends considerably out to sea to be an island, calling it the Isla de Cayyes.[a] When in sight of this the commander wished to reconnoiter it and we bore to the NW in order to enter a passage which this island seemed to form with the coast. When within two miles of it we sounded finding five fathoms. This unexpected piece of news produced great consternation, moving the geographer to reconnoiter from the mizzentop what formed a large bay at the bottom of which the coast was so low that the horizon was level with the water. It could only be made out that it was joined to the point, which seemed to be an island, by reason of the spray from the surf which the sea made on the beach. We immediately veered off to avoid the danger so near of running ashore and left the coast having reconnoitered and marked the so-called Isla de Kayyes which is not an island but a cape or point which extends far out to sea.[b]

I omit relating the events day by day from this time on, as I do not wish to commit errors touching the technical points in navigation, because although I endeavored to instruct myself more in such curious and instructive matters it did me no good, as it brought on a mysterious and studied silence of the officials and the pilots which reached the point of their not telling me anything the more I asked them. When they do tell me anything it is such that I am left with the same doubts. I will therefore say only what I know and heard accidentally.

We continued along the coast until we reached the foot of Mount San Elias, situated in 59° of latitude where the wind died out. The chain of mountains on the coast from Principe Guillermo to Nootka is certainly worthy of the most careful investigation by a learned naturalist. From the degrees of latitude 60° and 61° a remarkable elevation of the coast was observed above the level of the sea which it was noted rises from the profundity of the sea as in various places close to the coast we have found by sounding at some places a great depth and at others none. It is more remarkable that these mountains and hills for the greater part are of black stone like jet, therefore Nature manifests itself in these places in a very remarkable manner as the shape of the mountains are very extraordinary forming peaks and sharp points. In my opinion these places could not be traversed in traveling toward the interior. These observations gave place to very scientific reflections on the part of some of the persons on the ship. Don Tadeo Haenke is of two

[a] Called by Cook Kaye's Island, now known as Kayak.
[b] Vancouver later determined that it actually is an island.

opinions: in the first place he says that the solidity and consistency of the universe consists more in the rocks than in the earth, drawing the same comparison as Father Tosca[51] that the world is like a human body in which are indispensably placed bones and flesh for a greater firmness. The first furnish the framework and fundamentals and the second fills the vacancies. From this he infers that in this part of the world of which we are speaking greater firmness is necessary although ignorant of the reasons which might be the cause of this necessity, through which the wise Maker of all things has placed the skeleton in these parts and the soil farther south. He is further of this opinion on seeing that as we fall down in latitude the elevation of the coast also insensibly becomes lower, and there is a mixture of earth and rock. This admirable order of things which exists over thousands of leagues cannot be the mere child of accidents which can often be seen in Nature but that of Divine Providence who, with hidden and sapient ends, impenetrable to men, has determined all things. Among various mountains of this class there are some of gigantic magnitude such as the great mountain of San Elias, so named in a superlative degree by Captain Cook. By reason of having eight days of calm weather and being close to this mountain at a distance of a mile we could see it better than any of the voyagers before us.

Captain Cook placed the mountain twenty leagues inland and we observed it to be at the very edge of the water, with a difference that to the southeast there is a beach which stretches away to a distance of eight leagues to the foot of the high summits of the coast, which serves as a kind of step, and is covered with snow. To the northwest there is another piece of very elevated coast cut off perpendicularly and so equally that it forms a wall against whch the waves beat furiously. This ends in a point which looks to the south. After doubling this, other mountains are seen which lie behind in a second tier, where there seems to be some *ensenada,* river, or passage (which it all seemed to be), worth a scrupulous examination which perhaps would meet the glorious purpose of this voyage. This was not done, however, because the commander did not wish to do so, notwithstanding such opportune weather which we were enjoying and the fact that the officials were desirous of making this exploration in the longboat.

Between these two coasts, close to the coast itself lies the mountain of a formidable height and magnitude, totally covered with snow from its foot to its summit, and ending in a peak. Farther inside, and at the bottom of this *ensenada* or at the beginning of it, because the passage referred to is behind the first range of hills on the coast to the northwest, the size of it could not be made out. Almost at the summit a very large hollow was noticed with various gashes and declivities which reached down to the plain. During these eight days the geographer marked it to his full satisfaction from different points and I drew several views of it, one of them particularly exact which the geographer adopted for the collection.

The day before the wind came up with which we continued our voyage we anchored with a kedge anchor to prevent wearing out the crew, which was tired out with useless maneuvers because the light breezes which came up lasted for a very short time, and what ground was made in this way was lost through the currents which carried us towards the coast. This same afternoon we saw come out to visit us from the foot of the mountain behind the low coast which extends to the southeast a canoe in which was an Indian who lives in this neighborhood. Without any fear and boldly he came on board showing much pleasure and confidence and signified to us by signs that he had come to visit us to tell us that all his countrymen were ready to entertain us, and that for that purpose we should raise the kedge anchor and follow him and he would conduct us to a large port which was behind the point where they had their town and where they would trade with us for sea-otter skins. This information made us firmly of the opinion that we had formed that in this place there was something worth our reconnoitering, the more so, as we were close to Puerto Mulgrave and between Cabo Buen Tiempo and Principe Guillermo[a] which we had proposed to investigate. In this space we should explore carefully, foot by foot, for the desired strait of Ferrer Maldonado. Even if we were not successful in finding it there would at least be left the complete satisfaction that no one in the future could carry off this glory. Such considerations brought much grief to the pilots and some of the officers, among whom there exists a true appreciation of the honor and glory of the nation. The commander was also inspired with the same sentiments but he was whimsical and had formed the opinion that there was not and could not be any such strait. For this reason he did not wish to persist in scrupulously examining this piece of coast. Accordingly we sailed mostly at some distance from it. The Indian went away seeing that we did not wish to respond to his wishes leaving with us as a present some excellent

[a] That is, Cape Fairweather and Prince William Sound.

A plebeian

A plebeian woman of Port Mulgrave

An Indian armed for war of Port Mulgrave

A disagreement with the natives of Port Mulgrave, June 5, 1791

The Chief Ankaiui of Port Mulgrave

A woman of Port Mulgrave

Inhabitants of Port Mulgrave

Inhabitants of Port Mulgrave

fish and strawberries and the commander gave him in exchange some looking glasses, little bells, and beads for a large and beautiful sea-otter skin which he wore as a cape.

With some light winds which kept freshening we weighed the kedge anchor the following morning and sailed along close to the coast. That same afternoon we were in front of Cabo Buen Tiempo which has been described. All day many whales of all sizes accompanied us, giving us quite some diversion. Some of them were very large. The pilots say that when the fish in the sea are very lively and uneasy it is a sign of a storm. The next day we found that we had doubled the cape. We continued sailing along reconnoitering the coast and the most salient points.[52] This takes a direction to the ESE from the cape. By dead reckoning for two days and the N and NW wind which favored us we found that we had made two good days' run from Cabo de San Elias to the Puerto de los Remedios[53] in front of which we found ourselves. Already the snow in this neighborhood was diminishing and no more was noticed than some on the elevated peaks. In consequence the coast was very low, full of forests of high pines and undergrowth. From Cabo de Buen Tiempo to that of Engaño[a] we noticed many islands and small rocky islands quite close to the coast, which also might have been a worthy object of our explorations as well as the Estrecho de Aguilar[b] situated in 58° to the southeast of Cabo Buen Tiempo, although this last was more impracticable on account of the time necessary to explore a strait, which is quite a difficult problem, inasmuch as the current from it runs out very swiftly to the sea. All these days were foggy, obscure, and wet, and although we sailed along quite close to the coast we could not see more than a little of the beach on account of the fog and the low clouds which covered the surface of the mountains.

Near Cabo del Engaño at a distance of two miles the wind shifted to the E and that same night it settled around in the SE, very fresh and with more fog and darkness. It is to be noted that in these latitudes clear and limpid atmosphere is enjoyed always when the wind reigns N, NNW or NW, but to the surprise of all we experienced clouds and fog from Cabo Buen Tiempo to that of Engaño. It is also to be noted that along all this coast there is much sargasso and a marine plant like an orange with a long trunk the leaves of which are somewhat like those of the vine. This plant keeps all of its foliage when underneath the water

[a] Cabo Engaño, named by Bodega in 1775, now Cape Edgecumbe.
[b] Suría is here mistaken in the name. The Estrecho or Río de Aguilar was much farther south. He probably referred to Cross Sound.

but immediately withers when out of it. We collected some of it and found out by experiment what I have just set down. The botanist Haenke described them and added them to his Herbarium. Having passed so close to Cabo del Engaño we were able to recognize with all possible exactness the Ensenada del Susto[a] which is found after doubling the cape. We saw that it was very large, contained good shelter and much dense forest.

On the following morning the commander, fearful of some danger, determined to get ready for sailing as the wind had grown stronger and was contrary to our course thus making it impossible for us to approach the coast. In effect, we lost sight of it and in a short time discovered off the bow a large island. We went to look it over and they said what it was called but I do not remember.[b] We now discovered an archipelago of an infinite number of islands of different sizes which covered the whole horizon. We passed between them, marking them and reconnoitering them, and sailing among them for two days. These are in latitude 56°,[c] before reaching the famous Puerto de Bucareli,[54] which is in 55°. Up to this port and even beyond there is a countless multitude of these islands, the most noted one and which is beyond the said port and is remarkable for its size is the one named "Reina Carlotta" by the English.[55]

About 10 o'clock on the day following we again saw the coast and the sky cleared up a little. We directed ourselves to reconnoiter the entrance to the Entrada de Bucareli and at about 2 o'clock in the afternoon we were four miles distant from the port. We recognized the mouth of it, marking all the most interesting points and confirmed the maps of Don Juan Bodega y Quadra, and Mourelle,[56] his pilot, who laid the bases for this port. This was the reason why we did not engage carefully in this reconnaissance as we saw by their maps the care and exactness with which those deserving officers worked out this interesting point of geography. It may be said with propriety by way of note that this is the most famous port[57] in the world for its size and the number of innumerable sheltered ports, large and small, which surround it. To give a moderate idea of it the above mentioned surveys of our sailors, to which I refer the inquiring individual, is sufficient. These, notwithstanding, the two journeys which they made to it, employing two summers in this

[a] Sitka Sound.

[b] He probably means Biorka Island.

[c] He probably meant Coronation, Hazy Island and others. All along this coast Malaspina gave names to various openings which appear on his map but are not mentioned in any of the texts.

exploration and experiencing many sieges and dangers in treating with the natives who are very fierce and daring, never could ascertain its complete extension so spacious is it.

At 6 in the afternoon the wind died down when we were one mile distant from the most southern point of the port,[a] the beaches and the surf on the shore being very clearly visible. We were astonished at not seeing any canoe or signs of habitation or smoke as on the rest of the coast, which we were accustomed to see occasionally as a sign which they make to call the ships to trade for furs. The islands which we had to the west of us seemed to be more numerous than those of the preceding days because at sunset we saw in the west and on the horizon formed by the clouds themselves an extensive and perfect coast line with various islands, points, and bays, which by having lasted with a most unalterable shape for more than a half an hour caused the commander and the other officials to get out the geographical charts and prove by them whether or not it was land. When they were flattering themselves with having made some new discovery to add to their maps, they saw this fantasy marvellously losing its shape and disappearing until the horizon was quite clear and those which had been marked down were the only ones to be seen. What more conduced to our belief in this phenomenon was that when it occurred we were sailing at some distance from the coast in order to double the south point of Puerto Bucareli. If the calm had continued this coast could not have been reached from where we were stopped, even supposing that it was real.

Seeing the coast of this Puerto Bucareli so cut up into small islands, rocks, and farallons, besides the innumerable islands of this archipelago which we surmised to exist, gives us occasion to think with some foundation that in some other time perhaps this coast extended for a long distance into the sea and that through some formidable earthquake it sank, leaving behind the many islands. This opinion is more confirmed if you make two reflections: first, if we compare America with the other parts of the world, Asia, Africa, and Europe, it will be noted that America from the Strait of Bering in 72° of latitude north to 60° south, where Cape Horn is located, covers a tremendous distance of thousands of leagues which occupy almost half the globe, considering the fact that this extent of latitude is very unequal to its longitude, as there are various isthmuses, for example, that of Panama, where the distance between the north and south seas is only thirty

[a] Cape Felix.

leagues, America occupies a very small extent of longitude compared to that of the two immensely wide seas which bathe it. In the South Sea, as a proof of its size, the direct course from Acapulco to Manila, that is from the coast of America to that of Asia, measures 3000 leagues. That this disproportion which I have shown is notable in this part of the world and is not seen in the others is manifest by what I have said. Possibly in ancient times America was wider and who knows if it did not connect with Asia, when the distance from one to the other was much less, and that in consequence the many islands which are close to both coasts were united to them. It is noticeable that some of them, as for example Guadalupe, which is in front of Old California,[58] is fifty leagues distant from the coast, the Sandwich Islands[59] are distant a thousand leagues, and those of Otaeti[60] are the same, both settled by people. How could these people have come, lacking as they did a knowledge of navigation? On the other hand their language, customs, dress, and religion do not bear any resemblance to those of the uncivilized people of America. If their inhabitants had belonged to the cultivated nations of Europe who by some accident or shipwreck had reached these islands it is believable that there would not have remained some remnant at least of their primitive dialect? Is it not the fact that their language is original and different from all those known? If we reflect on their religion we encounter the same difficulty, as they are idolatrous like all the inhabitants of the northern regions of America, and if we enlarge somewhat on the matter, in view of the proofs just given, it can be considered that the havoc and ruin of this coast happened many centuries before the conquest. In view of the fact that in none of the writings of those times does any similar notice occur nor even by tradition of the Indians themselves, in my opinion, some continents became separated and lost when that terrible earthquake took place at the death of Jesus Christ, demonstrating even to a stubborn person the pain of seeing Our Maker suffer. Then would have been formed these islands, separating among them the inhabitants who before occupied the whole continent. For this reason little difference is noted in the customs of these islanders from that on this coast. Likewise, they are found to be heathen because when this event occurred all Americans were heathen, and many centuries were to pass before the Spaniards propagated among them the light of the evangel.

I must give some slight idea of a very great storm which, according to the expression of the commander, was the worst he had experienced in all the voyage from Cadiz, and it will serve to explain his own anxiety although he tried to hide it. The signs previously referred to of a great number of whales and other fish swimming about, jumping, and appearing on the surface awakened our vigilance, leading us to expect every instant a strong storm, as these signs are usually sure ones. Actually the wind came up from the SE so excessively strong that it was necessary to handle the ship with every care, furling the topgallant sails, the mainsail, and the foretopsail, and remaining only with the topsail and the foresail. The wind kept getting stronger every instant with rain and a very heavy sea. The rolls were tremendous and the darkness terrifying. This unfortunate event obliged us to stand off from the Isla Carlotta, which bore to the ESE in order to run before the wind for safety. Thus we ran for six days of terrific storm. If it had not been for the wonderful construction of our vessels, built purposely to withstand every class of danger we would without doubt have perished, as it seemed as if all the elements had conspired against us. There was not a man who could keep his footing, simply from the violence of the wind, so that besides the mountains of water and foam which swept over us, there arose from the surface of the water small drops of spray forming a strange and copious rainfall never before seen. The roaring noise of both elements was horrible and terrifying. The confusion and shouting on the ship, together with the maledictions of the sailors, who in such cases break out into blasphemy, augmented the terror to such an extent that it seemed as if all the machinery of the universe were ready to destroy us. During this time we suffered such inconveniences as cannot be described, for during the six days there was no one who could get repose for a moment. We weathered this storm with topgallantsails down and at times without any sail, although usually with the foresail. This bad weather lasted from the 2nd to the 8th of August. From 12 o'clock at night of the 8th the wind began to die down and at 12 midday of the 9th, it died down completely. The sea continued with almost the same force but some breezes from the northwest, which began to blow after the calm, and carried away all the fog and darkness, contributed very much to quieting it down, leaving the atmosphere clean and clear. The men were so worn out that the commander did not wish to repair the sails, some of which had been blown to pieces, and he simply ordered others to be substituted which had already been used so that we could continue on our course. As we were at some distance from the coast we could not see Cabo Boiset.[a]

[a] The present Cape Cook.

In order to thank the sailors for the good work they had done and at the same time to keep away from the scurvy which was insiduously threatening them, the first symptom of this perverse sickness being noted in the heaviness of their limbs, we began to give them lemonade on the advice of the surgeon Don Francisco Flores. It was also given to the officers and the other persons in the wardroom. The order was communicated to the *Atrevida* where they also began to put the same remedy into effect. From the 9th to the 10th we found that by dead reckoning we had made a very good day's run of eighty leagues, and having marked the point on our map we found that we were very close to Nootka. The desire of our commander to treat with the natives of this place, in view of the great things said about them by all travelers, Spaniards as well as Englishmen, as well as his wish to find out if this territory was an island and run the bases of the port because he considered the foreign maps to be incorrect, in view of their little concordance with ours, he took a course towards land, steering to the east with a west wind astern. At 11 in the morning we discovered the coast of Nootka and a little later marked the Punta de Tassis[61] which stood out behind the mountains. The first view of the coast indicated that it was low, because although mountains could be seen they were not very high. Their clearness or darkness made manifest their different locations which they had above the level of the sea. Various channels and lagoons, islands, farallons, small rocky islands could be made out with various points and low lands all covered with pine trees. It was all marked down and noted until at night we hove to for fear of striking on some shoal which without doubt we would have done if we headed into port.

On the 11th at 4 o'clock in the morning we continued along the coast and at this hour two canoes of Indians came close to us, but they could not get alongside and went away. The wind slackened a great deal so that we did not enter the channel at 12. At 3 in the afternoon we were becalmed and two other canoes came out, one of which came alongside, the Indians climbing up with much speed without any ladder. We noticed in them a great liveliness and an admirable behavior. The first thing they asked for was shells with this word *"pachitle conchi,"*[a] alternating this with saying *"Hispania Nutka"* and then words which meant alliance and friendship. We were astonished to hear out of their mouths Latin words such as Hispania, but we concluded that perhaps they had learned this word in their trading with

[a] This means "give us shells!"

Englishmen or that it was a bad pronunciation. That same afternoon near the entrance it became calm and it was now necessary to anchor with the kedge in 24 fathoms, sand bottom, in order to await another day, and with the east wind and by tacking to get in without danger in view of the fact that the entrance to the port is very narrow. In a little while a longboat could be seen rounding the point to the ENE which in two hours and with some labor reached us. In it were twenty sailors and the master. He told the commander that he had been sent by his Ensign, Don Pedro Saavedra,[62] who was then in the port, to assist us in whatever he could. The commander made them stay.

On the 12th at 8 o'clock in the morning we raised the kedge and crowded on all sail in order to enter the port. We anchored there with felicity in 8 fathoms, bottom sand, in front of the beach of the establishment and to the starboard of the frigate *Concepción* from San Blas which was under the command of Saavedra.[63]

The captain of the Company of Volunteers of Catalonia, Don Pedro Alberni,[64] as governor and castellan of the new establishment and fort, rendered us the corresponding salute and came aboard in his boat with Saavedra. The commander regaled them with a good breakfast. Immediately the small boats were put in the water and went ashore with two warps, with which and with two anchors we made everything safe. The port is not the most capacious and the entrance as stated above is very narrow. Two small vessels can scarcely sail out or enter it together. It makes a figure similar to this[a] aside from the many islands and farallons which are close to the coast. This drawing was made on the spot and immediately after the entrance. It lacks the final arrangement.

On the 13th the placing of the observatory was finished[65] and the commander arranged to send a request to the captain and chiefs of the tribes to come from their homes and treat with us for the purpose of acquiring the information which we solicited about their customs, dress, physiognomy, etc., and compare them in this way with the foreign accounts which we had with us. By means of some Indians who were paddling about in their canoes asking for shells, copper, and other things, we sent word to Macuina,[66] the head absolute chief of all this country and to Tlupanamibo,[67] his subordinate, and who acts at times as head of the army in their military exploits. From the beginning we noticed in the other Indians, the plebes who were roundabout, a

[a] Here is included a rough pen and ink sketch of the port which is not reproduced as there are many better plans.

submission to this chief so complete that in their conversations, whether it was because of recognizing that they were vassals, or on account of superstition, or some [the text breaks off here]. A small fruit like a black grape, bittersweet, which the botanist called beargrape. They were agreeable and pleasant to the taste and we continued eating them. We had commenced to trade in furs as we had found that the natives were losing their fear of us. They were approaching our vessels with more confidence but up to the present time the trade was not favorable because according to what they gave us to understand they were short of these skins because they had sold them to the Englishmen, Colnett[68] and Kemirrik (Kendrick),[69] who had visited them this year. Besides this the natives, that is the plebes, or as they are called *mischimis*, do not possess an abundance of these skins as do their chiefs or *taiyes* with whom for the present we have not agreed. The sea-otter skins which we have seen are inferior in quality to those of Mulgrave and Principe Guillermo. The same can be said of the fish although it is always of excellent quality.

About 10 in the morning we saw rounding the point inside the port which closes it and divides it from the channel, which leads to the settlements of the chiefs, a large canoe of different shape from the ordinary ones. It was manned by ten rowers on a side and in the middle was the chief named Tlupanamibo with a large square chest. He came aboard, confident and happy, all by himself. Through Captain Alberni and a Guadalajara boy[70] of the *Gertrudis* who served as interpreters we made out his harangue "Great chief, Tlupanamibo, *tasi* inferior to you, has heard your polite and friendly message and in compliance with it and with the friendship which I profess for your nation and the great chief who directs you to our habitations, I have come to see you and salute you. I persuade myself that you will be informed by Captain Alberni of the fidelity of my actions. He has experienced from me and my men through my command better actions than words. He is here and can tell you the truth. I begin with this discourse in order to gain your full confidence the same that I expect you will have in me. Do not believe that my years can serve as an obstacle to serve you in what you may be pleased to order me to do. Although you may marvel and believe me a barbarian I am not ignorant of the inviolable laws of friendship. They inspire me to tell you not to confide in nor to feel safe from the dissimulated perfidy of Macuina. I tell you that he is crafty and overbearing and he looks on you with hatred and abhorrence. He shortly meditates dislodging you from this place which you have founded in our dominion, but he cannot do it while Tlupanamibo lives, who, being experienced in this double-crossing game, will know how to oppose it as I have his malign projects up to the present. Although, as I am his subject, I could accompany him in his enterprises, I forbear to do it because my heart is filled with integrity and justice. I know that you are men like us but more civilized and united to the universal and particular interests of yourselves and your nation, on which account I do not admire your manufactures and productions so much esteemed amongst us. The plebes do not yet think and so they attribute to prodigies and enchantments those operations you perform for the management of your great canoes. Finally, if you wish to gain the entire confidence of all the tribe proceed like the English do, who although more greedy, are upright and unchangeable and their treatment of us is familiar and gracious."

This elegant speech was so specious that our officials formed an elevated conception of this tribe, but I do not admire them as I remember the elegant way in which the Mexicans know how to make a harangue.

[There is obviously a leaf or two missing here. What follows evidently occurred on the 15th and 16th. The leaf which is here appended refers to events which happened on the 13th and 14th.]

. . . of the many which they had. First they named it and then continued their narrative, this novelty being noticeable in each period. The same day we went on board the *Gertrudis* to honor Saavedra who after having regaled us with what he could told us all he knew about the country. Don Pedro Alberni, the distinguished official who will occupy one of the most worthy places in the account of this voyage on account of his skill and management of these natives, and who was charged with sustaining the establishment and keeping it free from invasions, also did the same. I reserve all these notices for the final description.

The chaplain[71] of the ship gave us six boys which he had obtained through industry and interest in exchange for guns. He had obtained them for the purpose of teaching them the catechism and instructing them in the doctrines of our sacred religion and then baptising them. His Christian charity gave us much satisfaction and stimulated us to follow his [re]commendable project. There was among them one whom the sailors called "Primo." He displayed quite a little vivacity and already could pronounce some words in our language. He told us that he had been destined to be a victim and to be eaten by Chief Macuina together with many others, and that this custom was practiced with the younger prisoners of war, as well as in the ceremonies which were used in such a detestable and horrible sacrifice.[72] Having discovered a way to escape he took refuge on the *Gertrudis*. This same day, when it was already night, two children arrived, a boy and a girl, brother and sister, who had also escaped from the fury of these barbarians. They said that they came from the country of the Nuchimas,[73] who inhabit the banks of a great lake seven suns distant from us, so they call their days.

On the 14th the pilots commenced to lay the bases for the port. The astronomers to make observations, and the sailors to repair some cables and construct a mast for the longboat, as the one which we had was broken, and it was necessary to equip the two longboats for the expedition which the commander contemplated during our stay in this port, and which was to be commanded by the two officers who had joined our vessels in Acapulco, having come from Spain by way of Vera Cruz, namely Don José Espinosa[74] and Don José Zevallos.[75] He wished to give these a chance to participate in the glories which others had gained by such commissions which being dangerous and adventurous were worthy of such honored offices.

The botanist, Don Tadeo Haenke, began to botanise. He made a collection of plants but very meager because he could not find in port other plants distinct from those in Europe. He did, however, find many anti-scorbutic plants classifying these as well as the pines of which there were many different species.

Every afternoon for a respite from our labors we went to walk on the beaches. These are composed of small stones of various kinds of marble and jasper, the greater part black, like all the coast. They were in spherical and elliptical form, very pleasing and for curiosity's sake all of them were collected. The forest close to these beaches is extremely thick. Nature is here observed in its rustic and rare state. It is necessary to travel through it with much care, as, during the course of years and the fact that the natives do not cultivate it, trees have been accumulating on top of each other.

Note

I have omitted the details about the *Ankau* of Mulgrave, his son, and some others until I can put these points in a fair copy without terror or undue inconvenience.

On the 17th we noticed that the natives were losing their fear which the outrage, that had been committed by Martinez,[76] had produced in them. Whenever those natives thought about him they displayed the most extreme desire for vengeance. They now approached us with familiarity and assured us that their principal *tais* or chief would come to visit us. The noble Tlupanamibo was lodged on the beach at the establishment where at certain hours of the day he sang for us in company with his oarsmen about the glories of his nation and his ancestors, and at other times about his own feats and military exploits, all in a meter like the anacreontic. When he got to these last songs this old man took on such vigor and enthusiasm that he was able to represent perfectly with his actions the struggles, the leaping, and dismay of his enemies and all that could give a true idea of his particular triumphs.   At 4:30 in the afternoon he prepared his canoe for his return, leaving as a hostage a son of his and the square box until his return with the Emperor Macuina. He went way with great swiftness. I drew a portrait of him which was much praised for its likeness to him in his features. This day the commander gave an order that at midnight the two longboats should set sail and make a reconnaissance by way of the channels which lead to the establishments of the Emperor Macuina. They were well manned with sailors and soldiers to the number of thirty-two, sixteen in each of the two longboats. Also in each one were placed two swivel guns, the corresponding ammunition and provisions and all the instructions which were to be opened at the foot of Mount Tassis. So at 11:15 everything was ready and Don José Cevallos and Don José Espinosa were already on board.   At this time I begged the commander to distinguish me by appointing me to such a glorious small expedition. He granted my request, providing me with a gun, pistols, and ammunition as if I were a soldier, adding the instruments necessary for the operation of the business which I was to undertake. With shouts and acclamations we departed from the corvettes and commenced by rowing because there was calm. We steered for the middle of the principal channel which bears to the NNE.[77] Considering that we lacked wind for sailing it was necessary to avail ourselves of our oars. This channel narrowed in an uncomfortable way, in some places it was wider and in others narrower, and large vessels, such as brigantines and schooners, could not make use of it.[78] [Two indistinguishable words at the end of the page begin a new sentence which is not continued on any of the other leaves.][a]

[a] Suría erred in writing the names of some individuals referred to toward the end of the narrative. Saavedra's name was Ramón, instead of Pedro, and Cevallos', Ciriaco, instead of José. The Indian he calls Tlupanamibo was known by other names, all quite different from this. The Spaniards usually called him Clupananul. It has now been shortened to Tlupana.

FOOTNOTES TO BE ADDED TO WAGNER'S TRANSLATION
By Dr. Donald C. Cutter

1. José Bustamante y Guerra was born in 1759 at Ontaneda, Santander. He became a midshipman at the Naval School at Cádiz in 1770. After the end of this expedition he was subsequently elevated to Brigadier, roughly rear admiral. He served subsequently as Governor of Uruguay and later as Captain General of Guatemala (1810-1819). He died in Madrid in 1825.

2. The prestigious order of Sántiago was founded in the Kingdom of León in 1116 and served to protect pilgrims going to Santiago de Compostela from Moslem attacks. Admission to this and other military orders required purity of blood, nobility of lineage, and meritorious service.

3. Luis Neé was hardly a "very famous Frenchman," but was an experienced botanist. Before the expedition this French-born, naturalized Spaniard was Professor of Botany and Chief Gardener of the Royal Apothecary. He had botanized extensively throughout much of Spain, but particularly in the mountains of Asturias "for twenty years." He was the founder of the Botanical Garden of Pamplona. Malaspina documents, MS 2296 in Museo Naval. Luis Neé did not go to the Northwest Coast but stayed in Mexico to gather specimens. However, he made scientific descriptions of botanical items gathered for him by his colleagues, including two species of California oak named after him. His more highly trained colleague, Dr. Tadeo Haenke, referred to Neé as "a mere gardener."

4. Not included in the Wagner publication.

5. Suría did not go along to San Blas, but rather stayed in Acapulco.

6. The Fort of San Diego de Acapulco. The *Figure* mentioned in the journal is not included in Wagner's work.

7. Antonio Pineda, Chief of Natural History of the expedition and born in Guatemala, was not first lieutenant of marines as Wagner translated his commission. He was a senior grade lieutenant in the Spanish Navy *(Marina)*. His activity is treated extensively in Iris Higbee Wilson, "El Coronel don Antonio de Pineda y su viaje mundial," in *Revista de Historia Militar*, No. 15, 1964. Suría worked with Pineda for a month, but Pineda also remained in Mexico during the Northwest Coast phase of operations. He died during the expedition's stay in the Philippine Islands and was buried there.

8. "Lista de dibujos concluidos...dibujado por Suría," in Pineda, Nueva Espana, MS 563 in Museo Naval.

9. The Tropic of Cancer is 23° 27' north latitude.

10. Cayetano Valdés y Flores Bazán was born in Sevilla in 1767 and became a midshipman at Cádiz in 1781. He left the main expedition after the visit to the Northwest Coast in order

to command the *Mexicana* in the voyage of two Spanish sloops which made the first circumnavigation of Vancouver Island in 1792. His varied later life included ten years of exile in England and the position of Captain General of the Navy. He died in 1834.

11. Felix Fontana, Italian physiologist, born in 1730, was the author of various works including *Descrizioni ed usi di alcuni instrumenti per misurar la salubrità dell' aria (Florence, 1774.).*

12. Lieutenant Secundino Salamanca came aboard at Acapulco. He served as second in command under Dionisio Alcalá-Galiano on the sloop *Sutil* in 1792 in the circumnavigation of Vancouver Island. Salamanca retired in 1803 as a commander.

13. Rafael de Arias was supply officer on the *Descubierta*, but also helped with botany and as a scribe.

14. Suría's spelling of Haenke's name. For extensive treatment of this versatile member of the expedition and his activity see: Laurio H. Destefani and Donald Cutter, *Tadeo Haenke y el final de una vieja polémica,* (Buenos Aires, 1965).

15. Fabio Aliponzoni, like Malaspina an Italian, joined the expedition as a midshipman.

16. The father chaplain was Francisco de Paula Aniño and the surgeon was Pedro María González.

17. Juan Maqueda was a pilot aboard the *Descubierta*. He left the group later in the Philippine Islands.

18. Really 32⁰.

18. Really 32^0.

19. The doctor was Flores and his assistant, Don Tadeo Haenke.

20. Suría was the only one to comment on the weather being in any way unusual.

21. San Lucar de Barrameda.

22. Juan Francisco de la Bodega y Quadra Mollinedo had been born of Basque parents in Lima, Peru in 1743. He enlisted at the age of 19. In 1776 he had explored the coast in the *Sonora*. Subsequently he played a major role in the Nootka Sound controversy as Spanish Commissioner to meet with English Captain George Vancouver. He served for a while as Commanding Officer of the Spanish Naval Department of San Blas and died in that position in 1794. Details of his life are found in Michael E. Thurman, *The Naval Department of San Blas: New Spain's Bastion for Alta California and Nootka, 1767-1798* (Glendale, California, 1967). Suría calls him Quadra, as did the English and many Spaniards. He was more appropriately Bodega or Bodega y Quadra.

23. Felipe Bauzá y Cañas was born in Palma de Mallorca and was already a combat veteran and a mapmaker of merit. He later became a captain. He also spent ten years in exile in London and died there in 1834. At the time he was recruited for the expedition he was a teacher of fortification and drawing at the Naval School at Cádiz.

24. The position as determined by Bauzá and Maqueda was quite exact at 57⁰ north latitude. Wagner in his translation continually used the expression "mark," for the Spanish "marcar," to mean "to take a bearing on" or "observe." The reader should then mentally translate Wagner's "mark" in such a way.

25. Cape Edgecumbe.

26. Queen Charlotte Island, so named by the English Captain George Dixon for his vessel.

27. Coastal profiles were done of both Cape Fairweather and Mount Fairweather (Buen Tiempo) which views still exist in the Museo Naval. The climax peak is 15,320 feet in elevation and is in roughly 59⁰ north and 138⁰ west.

28. Named for Constantine John Phipps, Second Baron of Mulgrave who had been Lord of the British Admiralty, 1777-82. Phipps Peninsula was given as Dixon's name for the mainland area west of Port Mulgrave. The larger bay is that of Yakutat of which Mulgrave forms a small part.

29. The year for Lorenzo Ferrer Maldonado's supposed voyage was 1588.

30. George Dixon (circa 1755-1800 had been an officer on Captain Cook's third expedition. Subsequently in 1787 he explored the Northwest Coast in the service of the King George's Sound Company of London aboard the *Queen Charlotte*. He published an account as *A Voyage round the world, but more particularly to the Northwest Coast of America* (London, 1789).

31. Point Turner on Khantaak Island was named for James Turner, second mate of Dixon's vessel.

32. The Malaspina observatory tent figures in several expedition drawings.

33. Plate V.

34. Frederica de Laguna in *Under Mount Saint Elias: The History and Culture of the Yakutat Tlingit* (Washington, 1972), p. 145, suggests a monster rat or even a raven.

35. Antonio de Tova Arredondo (not Tovar) was second in command of the *Atrevida*. He was born in 1760 in Santander Province. He kept an account of the voyage, the original of which is in the Municipal Library of Santander. By 1822 he was a Brigadier and serving as Port Director in his home port.

36. De Laguna suggests that the incident occurred on Khantaak Island, *Under Mount Saint Elias*, p. 150.

37. Today called Disenchantment Bay and Bancas Point. According to Tova who was there at the time the paper read: "The Corvettes of his Majesty Descubierta and Atrevida commanded by Don Alejandro Malaspina and Don José Bustamante discovered this port on the 20th of June 1791 and called it Desengaño, taking possession of it in the name of his Catholic Majesty."

38. De Laguna, *Under Mount Saint Elias*, p. 149, suggests that the sailor saw Russell Fiord on his long, cold trip.

39. Juan Bernaci was Lieutenant Juan Vernaci who became a midshipman in 1780. Later he was second in command of the *Mexicana* under Alcalá-Galiano in the 1792 circumnavigation of Vancouver Island. He died in Manila in 1810 as a Commander.

40. Wagner must have misread the Spanish here, since the incident clearly depicted in a drawing by José Cardero shows that it was a pair of trousers that had been stolen and were being returned. *Cabron* (he-goat) and *calzon* (trousers) could be confused, but the former makes no sense in context. De Laguna erroneously credits Suria with drawing this scene, as well as other scenes though several were actually signed by Cardero.

41. Official sources say that the lost crewman was Manuel Fernández, a marine gunner.

42. These are now in the Museo de América, Madrid.

43. These burials were on Phipps Peninsula where the party seems to have arrived via Anaku Inlet, a stream or body of water that almost makes the peninsula an island.

44. Cardero drew this scene of a house.

45. Expedition members compiled a rather substantial word list at Mulgrave.

46. Wagner made an error in translating here. The text reads "a mi no me parezen tales," and a substitute translation should read "and some islands according to what the pilots said, but to me there didn't seem to be any."

47. Antonia Valdés y Bazán.

48. Juan Sánchez was really José María Sánchez, second pilot of the *Descubierta*. He left the group in Manila due to ill health.

49. Glacial Sea is Arctic Ocean, and the South Sea is the Pacific Ocean.

50. Unalaska.

51. Father Tomás Vicente Tosca, born in Valencia in 1651, was a mathematician, architect, philosopher and physicist. He was the author of many works in both Spanish and Latin. He died in 1723.

52. Coastal profiles were drawn including one set of 33 which still exists in the Museo Naval. Spanish names were given to the coastal areas such as Ensenada de Castilla, Entrada de Aragón, Bahía de Palma, Ensenada de la Cruz [Cross Sound], Valle de Ruesga, Punta Barrigón, Cabo Español, Entrada de Granada, Entrada de Guadarrama, Puerto de Príncipe, etc.

53. Puerto de los Remedios was the name given by Bodega y Quadra for what is today Salisbury Sound at the north end of Kruzof Island.

54. Today Bucareli Bay, named in honor of Antonio María Bucareli y Ursúa, Viceroy of New Spain (1771-1779), and located in 55° 15' north latitude. Wagner mistranslates "famoso" which in this context means "spacious" and therefore "worthy of fame," but not necessarily well-known.

55. Queen Charlotte.

56. Francisco Antonio Mourelle, who became a Pacific Ocean explorer, and went on to great fame. He is the subject of a biography by Amancio Landin Carrasco, *Mourelle de la Rua, explorador del Pácifico,* (Madrid, 1971).

57. Again not "famous," but worthy of fame or appropriate.

58. Lower California.

59. Hawaiian Islands.

60. Tahiti.

61. This should probably read Tassis Peak, not Tassis Point, for the mountain is a prominent landmark on Vancouver Island, standing inland from Friendly Cove.

62. Ensign Don Pedro Saavedra was really Ramón Saavedra y Giraldez.

63. Saavedra was from Lugo, a knight of the order of Santiago. He was senior naval officer present at Nootka, commanding the 400 ton Frigate *Concepción* which was the station ship at that port.

64. The career of Pedro Alberni and the activiity of the company under his command is treated in Joseph Sanchez, "The Catalonian Volunteers in New Spain," Ph.D. dissertation, University of New Mexico, 1974. Alberni's service record is available in Archivo General de Simancas, Hojas Militares, legajo 7277. Alberni after his service at Nootka later became commandant of arms and interim governor of California, where he died in 1803. Alberni Canal and Port Alberni on Vancover Island are named for him.

65. Established on the beach at the south end of the Spanish settlement.

66. Maquinna or Macuina was principal chief of the Nootkans at the time of the Spanish occupation. He was the subject of frequent inquiry by Europeans and Americans. His likeness was drawn by Suría, as well as by other visiting artists.

67. Tlupanamibo or Tlupanululg was a subordinate chieftan with his rancheria on Tlupana Arm of Nootka Sound. He was also drawn in a pencil sketch by Suría.

68. James Colnett, a half-pay British naval officer, was the cause célèbre of the Nootka Sound Affair, having been taken prisoner by the Spanish. Both his ships and men were seized there in 1789.

69. John Kendrick, Sr. was about as anti-British as one could be. During the American Revolution he had been a privateer, preying on English shipping. At Nootka Kendrick supported the Spanish pretensions with great enthusiasm. He was a favorite trading partner of the Nootkans. After prolonged activity on the Northwest Coast he went on to Hawaii where he died in a freak accident. His son, Juan (John, Jr.) served for a while as a pilot in the Spanish naval service operating out of San Blas.

70. The "Guadalajara boy" may have been Gabriel del Castillo, a corporal of dragoons who was "interpreter." Archivo General de la Nación (Mexico), Marina, tomo 78.

71. The chaplain was Father Nicolás Loera (sometimes spelled as Luera), one of the seven chaplains assigned to the Naval Department of San Blas, Estado General...del Puerto de San Blas, June 20, 1792 in Archivo General de la Nación, Marina, tomo 87.

72. It was never proved conclusively that Maquinna practiced either ceremonial or dietary cannibalism, though he was charged with both, and such charges were investigated.

73. Warren Cook in *Floodtide of Empire,* p. 314, identifies the Nuchimas as the Kwakiutl.

74. José Espinosa y Tello was born in Sevilla in 1763. Before the expedition he had drawn maps of the northern coast of Spain. He later served as head of the Hydrographic Office and ascended to the rank of Lieutenant General of the Navy.

75. Ciriaco Ceballos (called by Suría José Zeballos) was born in Quijano in the mountains of Santander. He joined the Malaspina group in Acapulco. Years later he headed a hydrographic survey of the Gulf Coast of Yucatan and Campeche. As a full captain he died in Mexico during the war for independence, probably in 1810.

76. Estevan José Martínez had earlier caused a break in good Nootka-Spanish relations in an incident involving the killing of Nootka sub-chief Callicum. It was also Martínez who took Colnett prisoner, triggering the controversy with England. For aspects of his contribution to Pacific Northwest Coast history including biographical information, see: Roberto Barreiro-Meiro (ed.), *Estevan José Martínez, 1742-1798,* Vol. VI of *Colección de diarios y relaciones para la historia de los viajes y descubrimientos,* (Madrid, 1964).

77. Cook Channel, between Nootka Island and Bligh Island with its smaller adjacent isles known as the Spanish Pilot Group.

78. This detachment with which Suría went out became the first to circumnavigate Nootka Island.

COLOPHON

The *Tomás de Suría*, Voyage With Malaspina—1791, *was printed in the workshop of one Glen Adams, which is located in the quiet country village of Fairfield, Washington, in southern Spokane County. Type for this edition was keyboarded by Miss Bobi Pearson in twelve point Baskerville type, using a Compugraphic 48 computer photosetter. Page numbers are in twelve point Baskerville Bold and running heads in ten point Baskerville Bold. The photoset pages were printed with no enlargement of the Baskerville type. The paper stock is seventy pound Simpson Opaque offset. Binding is by William Bosch, Spokane. Camera-darkroom work was by Evelyn Clausen. The sheets were printed on a 770CD Hamada offset press operated by Don Cox. Indexing is by Edward J. Kowrach. General book design, also letterpress printing in color, is by Glen Adams. Stripping was done by Evelyn Clausen. Folding and assembly work was by Evelyn Clausen and Angela Wolf. A very considerable amount of assistance was given by Dr. Donald Cutter of the History Department of the University of New Mexico, Albuquerque, who footnoted the text and made numerous corrections of Spanish words and references. The Suría was originally printed in 1936 in an edition of a hundred copies, apparently an offprint of the periodical printing of that year. The Suría in this edition is not perfect but we made a valiant effort, we tried, and in trying we developed respect for the Spanish commanders who explored and charted the Northwest Coast in the late 1700's.*